8/02

D0986308

THE ANTIQUATED RIGHT

TEACHING TEXTS IN LAW AND POLITICS

David A. Schultz
General Editor

Vol. 18

PETER LANG
New York • Washington, D.C./Baltimore • Bern
Frankfurt am Main • Berlin • Brussels • Vienna • Oxford

Andrew Carlson

THE ANTIQUATED RIGHT

An Argument for the Repeal of the Second Amendment

PETER LANG
New York • Washington, D.C./Baltimore • Bern
Frankfurt am Main • Berlin • Brussels • Vienna • Oxford

Library of Congress Cataloging-in-Publication Data

Carlson, Andrew.
The antiquated right: an argument for the repeal
of the Second Amendment / Andrew Carlson.
p. cm. — (Teaching texts in law and politics; vol. 18)
Includes bibliographical references and index.
1. Firearms—Law and legislation—United States. 2. United States.
Constitution. 2nd Amendment. I. Title. II. Series.
KF3941 .C37   344.73'0533—dc21   2001038814
ISBN 0-8204-5666-7
ISSN 1083-3447

Die Deutsche Bibliothek-CIP-Einheitsaufnahme

Carlson, Andrew:
The antiquated right: an argument for the repeal
of the second amendment / Andrew Carlson.
−New York; Washington, D.C./Baltimore; Bern;
Frankfurt am Main; Berlin; Brussels; Vienna; Oxford: Lang.
(Teaching texts in law and politics; Vol. 18)
ISBN 0-8204-5666-7

Cover art by Mark Nelson
Cover design by Jacqueline Pavlovic

The paper in this book meets the guidelines for permanence and durability
of the Committee on Production Guidelines for Book Longevity
of the Council of Library Resources.

© 2002 Peter Lang Publishing, Inc., New York

Printed in the United States of America

CONTENTS

PREFACE

Gun control and the regulation of firearms occupy a central yet contentious place in contemporary American public policy debate. Whether prompted by juvenile violence in schools or efforts to reduce violent street crime, a desire to reduce domestic violence or to press the war on drugs, advocates and opponents of gun control have made guns a focal point of public discussion.

Yet this debate has become mired within another argument, a constitutional argument over the Second Amendment. While its words are few—A well-regulated militia, being necessary to the security of a free state, the right of the people to keep and bear arms, shall not be infringed—the cryptic and odd phrasing of the Second Amendment has transformed the debate over guns and gun violence in the United States into a constitutional fight over the proper meaning and interpretation of a portion of the Bill of Rights.

For some the right to bear arms guarantees a fundamental right of individuals to own guns, while others assert the Second Amendment speaks to a collective right to arm a militia. Still others assert that regardless of the intent of the Second Amendment's framers, the Constitution and its amendments are living documents that need to be interpreted in light of contemporary social values, needs, and circumstances.

The Antiquated Right boldly asserts that much of this debate is irrelevant. Andrew Carlson advocates divorcing the gun control debate from its constitutional politics through a repeal of the Second Amendment. Although he does not take a stand on gun control or regulation, Carlson makes a powerful case that repeal of this amendment would free social policy from the added confusion and problems that constitutionalizing this debate has produced.

Alexis de Tocqueville is widely quoted as asserting that: "There is hardly a political question in the United States which does not sooner or later turn into a judicial one. Consequently the language of every-day party-political controversy has to be borrowed from legal phraseology and conceptions." The debate over guns in the United States is perhaps the singularly best example of how law and politics have become intertwined. By advocating the return of this issue to democratically elected legislators who can examine guns from the vantage point of the public good, rather than from the perspective of judges interpreting the Constitution, *The Antiquated Right* represents an effort to reject Tocqueville's observations.

The Antiquated Right's conclusions are controversial. Yet, this book represents the type of scholarship I have sought to publish in Peter Lang's two series, Studies in Law and Politics and Teaching Texts in Law and Politics: scholarly, contentious work that addresses significant public policy and intellectual issues, written in a manner accessible both to legal scholars and students in the classroom.

David Schultz, Editor,
Studies in Law and Politics and
Teaching Texts in Law and Politics;
Professor, Hamline University

Introduction

> A well regulated Militia, being necessary to the security of a free
> State, the right of the people to keep and bear Arms, shall not be
> infringed.
>
> Second Amendment to the United States Constitution

With over 30,000 Americans dying every year from gunshot wounds,
the United States is embroiled in a debate about guns.[1] Should people
be allowed to own guns? What sorts of guns should be permitted?
What sorts of ammunition? What should someone have to do to buy
a gun? Should guns be registered? Participants on all sides of the debate agree levels of gun violence in the United States are intolerably
high—of the annual gun deaths, around 12,000 are homicides, the rest
being suicides and accidental deaths.[2] The debate concerns how best to
confront this problem. One school of thought holds that criminals
will always be able to get hold of guns. Law-abiding citizens should
therefore be permitted, or even encouraged, to own guns, on the reasoning that a populace capable of defending itself with deadly force
will deter all sorts of crime. The opposing school of thought maintains that, if fewer guns are in circulation, fewer guns will fall into the
hands of criminals, so gun crime will decrease. Strict controls should
therefore be placed on the purchase, ownership, and use of guns. Both
arguments have a coherent logic to them, and representatives of both
positions can produce reams of statistical evidence to support their

views. The gun debate often gets heated due to the extreme urgency
of the problem, and key facts are regularly misunderstood or distorted.
But this is how public policy gets made in a democracy: both sides put
forth their best arguments, challenge each other's claims, and perhaps
offer some compromises. In the end, a decision is reached on the basis
of majority rule, though usually reflecting some sort of compromise
with the dissenting minority.

Unfortunately, the public policy debate on guns often gets side-
tracked from the crucial question of how best to reduce gun violence.
This happens when gun advocates point out that the Second Amendment guarantees the right of the people to keep and bear arms, thus
rendering any proposed restrictions on guns not just bad policy but
unconstitutional. Proponents of gun control must then respond that
the Second Amendment merely grants states the collective right to
form militias; it was never intended to guarantee an individual right to
bear arms. Or, if an individual right is conceded, the debate shifts to
whether this right merely covers guns that could be used for militia
service, or whether it extends to all guns, including those owned for
such purposes as target shooting, hunting, collecting, and self-defense.
I say this turn in the debate is unfortunate, not because I believe public
discussion of the Constitution a bad thing—on the contrary, serious
constitutional debate is vital to a healthy democracy. But the constitutional debate is unfortunate in this case because it distracts people
from the pressing public policy discussion of how best to reduce gun
violence, while raising passions to a level where objectivity is lost and
compromise is scarcely possible. And all of this when gun policy
should not be a constitutional issue, at all.

Every well-organized state has a two-tiered system of laws. Constitutional laws are far-reaching in scope, relatively few in number,
and difficult to amend. They lay down the fundamental principles and
values intended to shape the political structure and character of the
state. Statutory laws are more detailed, numerous, and fluid. They
regulate the everyday administration of the state and the conduct of
its people, attempting to realize the state's ideals within the complex,
ever-changing empirical world. When the Bill of Rights was drafted in
1789, its framers had good reason to include the Second Amendment
among the ten amendments ultimately ratified. Whatever else it may
do, the Second Amendment was clearly intended to ensure the ability
of the young states to form militias. Most of the framers were of

English stock, and England had long been ruled by kings, some of whom had tried to assume the power of absolute monarchs. English kings never managed to rule as absolutely as their counterparts on the European continent, however, in part due to the English institution of the citizen militia. Composed of every able-bodied male reporting for service privately armed, the militia provided the king with a cheap means of national defense but also placed a check on royal power by serving as a counterweight to the professional army the king commanded more directly. When the American colonists, having endured years of oppressive colonial rule, finally broke out in revolution, they were seeking to free themselves, not just from George III, but from any sort of absolute governance. Accordingly, when the framers of the Second Amendment later provided constitutional protection for the state militias, they were trying to ensure that the federal government could never tyrannize the states the way the British government had tyrannized the colonies. The Second Amendment therefore helped shape both the political structure and character of the young United States, adding one more check to the system of checks and balances already established by the Constitution, while shouting out the governing ideal of the new country: "We will not abide tyranny!"

I imagine every American would still heartily second this proclamation. The Second Amendment, however, no longer makes the statement it once did, for times have changed, and the state militias no longer serve as a relevant or effective check against federal tyranny. For one thing, as America's democratic institutions have endured and matured over two centuries, a democratic culture has developed in the United States which is so strong that a slide into tyranny is hardly conceivable anymore. Hence, the need for state militias to serve as a "last resort" check on the federal government has greatly diminished. And if the federal government should ever try to tyrannize over the states, the militias will not be the force to stop it. The states no longer even have militias in the sense understood by the framers, citizen armies composed of every able-bodied male, privately armed. Nor is a revival of the militia likely, since it could no longer fulfill its traditional primary role of defending the country against foreign invasion and domestic insurgency—military weaponry has become so powerful, complex, and expensive that the United States has no choice but to rely on the professional military for its defense. But these advances in military technology also mean that if the federal government were ever to decide to oppress the country, citizens armed with rifles could do little to resist militarily. Yet, America is not therefore destined to fall under tyrannical rule, for modern peoples have developed other, less violent means of resisting oppressive governments, including boycotts, strikes, civil disobedience, and street demonstrations. Hence, the Second Amendment was good constitutional law in its time, but it has become obsolete. As I will argue, it should be repealed, in the interest of keeping the Constitution strong by removing a provision that no longer serves any constitutional purpose, while disrupting the contemporary public policy debate about guns.

Of course, those who do not interpret the Second Amendment as restricting the right to bear arms to the context of militia service will grant neither that the Second Amendment is outdated, nor that it is out of place in the contemporary gun debate. We must therefore ask whether the Second Amendment may be reasonably interpreted as guaranteeing an unrestricted individual right to bear arms. The strongest argument for this interpretation holds that the right to bear arms is an inalienable, natural right, springing from our natural right to self-defense. Because we possess natural rights even before we enter civil society, a constitution cannot *confer* such rights; it can only *guarantee* them, or protect them against infringement by the state. This explains the language of the Second Amendment, which proclaims that the right to bear arms "shall not be infringed." Yet, if the framers intended to guarantee a right to bear arms *for self-defense*, they were in error, for careful analysis of the concept of natural right shows that the right to bear arms for self-defense is not a natural right. It is rather a natural freedom we can perfectly well give up, along with other freedoms, when we agree to the social contract and enter civil society. Moreover, I will argue, a constitutionally conferred right to bear arms for the sake of self-defense would be bad constitutional law. When policy makers confront the problem of gun violence, they have two basic options for trying to enhance public safety: encouraging legal gun ownership to deter crime, or enacting gun controls to reduce the number of guns in circulation. Which strategy will work best in any given setting depends on innumerable empirical factors, which may well change over time. To tie the hands of policy makers by constitutionally depriving them of one of two possible responses to a public safety problem would contradict the very social contract, for in some instances it may prevent policy makers from taking steps that would demonstrably improve public safety. Only statutory laws have the flexibility and specificity needed to deal with public policy issues as fluid and complex as gun violence, so the proper forum for the gun debate is that of statutory, not constitutional, law. Thus, if the framers intended to guarantee an unrestricted individual right to bear arms in the Second Amendment, thus making public safety policy concerning about guns a constitutional issue, this was a mistake and provides one further argument for repeal.

To make the arguments I have just sketched out, I begin in Chapter 1 with a more detailed examination of the distinction between constitutional and statutory law. The subsequent three chapters establish the historical backdrop against which the Second Amendment was drafted. Chapter 2 explores the origins of the right to bear arms in England, while Chapter 3 traces out some developments in English political philosophy that came to underlie the American Constitution, with emphasis on the concepts of natural right and the social contract. Chapter 4 examines key events in the American colonies and the young United States that led up to the ratification of the Second Amendment. The historical groundwork having been laid, Chapter 5 summarizes the contemporary debate concerning interpretation of the Second Amendment and lays out a strategy for evaluating various interpretations. Chapter 6, focusing on interpretations that restrict the right to bear arms to a militia context, argues that the Second Amendment was a wise constitutional provision in its time, but it has become obsolete and therefore should be repealed. Chapter 7 asks whether the Second Amendment might invoke a completely unrestricted right to bear arms or a more restricted right to bear arms for self-defense but concludes that any such a provision would make bad constitutional sense. Finally, Chapter 8 draws all these arguments together and makes the final case for repeal of the Second Amendment.

Viewed in terms of the contemporary gun debate, the arguments in this book will likely appear to come from the side of gun control. And, no doubt, repeal of the Second Amendment will sound more appealing to proponents of gun control than to advocates of legal gun ownership. Yet, it must be stressed that, in this book, I do not take any position on the public policy question of what, if any, restrictions should be placed on the purchase, ownership, or use of guns. I certainly do not advocate a constitutional ban on guns—I believe this would be as misguided as a constitutional right to bear arms for self-defense. For what it is worth, I personally think some sort of compromise approach to the problem of gun violence needs to be worked out, such as permitting private gun ownership but stepping up registration requirements. In this book, however, my sole argument is that the proper forum for the gun debate is that of statutory law, not constitutional law. The Second Amendment disrupts the public policy debate about guns by improperly steering it into the constitutional sphere, even as it fails to perform any meaningful constitutional function, so I believe it should be repealed. Repeal of the Second Amendment would not prejudice the public policy debate on guns one way or the other. Rather, it would allow the debate to proceed unhindered by constitutional distractions, such that both sides could freely put forth their ideas, arguments, statistics, and proposals as we all work toward the common goal of reducing gun violence.

CHAPTER 1

Constitutional and Statutory Law

This book argues that the Second Amendment was good constitutional law when it was written, but it has become outdated and that the proper forum for the contemporary gun debate is the sphere of statutory, not constitutional, law. Hence, the first thing that must be done is to establish the distinction between constitutional and statutory law.

Two Types of Law

States have been drafting law codes at least since Hammurabi compiled the laws of Babylon and had them engraved on a column of black diorite some eighteen centuries before Christ. His express purpose in writing out these laws and putting them on public display was to ensure that the law, not the whims of any particular ruler, be sovereign. The city-states of ancient Greece were the first to draft constitutions, thus giving rise to the distinction between constitutional and statutory law. Since then, states have emphasized this distinction to varying degrees, sometimes sharply distinguishing the two types of law, sometimes allowing them to blend into one another. The distinction between constitutional and statutory law will therefore have different

implications in different states. Nevertheless, a general account of it
may be given.

Statutory laws provide for the everyday administration of the
state and regulate the conduct of its people. That military pension
checks are issued on the first Friday of the month, cars must drive on
the right side of the road, and burglary is punishable by ten years in
prison are all statutory laws. Concerning themselves with the details
of everyday life in the state, statutory laws are both numerous and
complex, for life has many details. Statutory laws also need to be
fairly fluid in nature. The everyday world is in a constant state of
change, so it must be possible to enact, revise, and repeal statutory
laws with relative brevity. Finally, given their subject matter, statutory laws tend to be guided in their development more by empirical
facts than abstract principles. For instance, that industrialized countries began enacting driving restrictions near the beginning of the
twentieth century was not because some political philosopher had
proclaimed these to be necessary for the free state. It was because the
horseless carriage was fast becoming a part of everyday life in the industrialized world.

Greek lawmakers realized, however, that if all a state's laws simply reflect the changing empirical world, both the state and its laws
will end up as confused and disjointed as everyday life tends to be. If
the state is to enjoy a stability, coherence, and unity, it must receive
guidance from some higher realm—a realm that stands above the vi-
cissitudes of everyday life and is guided more by abstract principles
than empirical details. This is the realm of constitutional law. Ever
since the Greeks started drafting constitutions, constitutions have
been viewed as forming a sort of "higher law," sometimes to the point
that they are granted almost a mystical or sacred status. One way constitutional laws remain above the flux of everyday life is that they are
typically more difficult to amend than statutory provisions. In the
United States, for instance, passage of a federal statutory law requires
a simple majority in both houses of Congress plus the signature of the
President. A constitutional amendment, on the other hand, requires a
two-thirds majority in both houses, plus ratification by the legislatures
of three-fourths of the states.[1] More importantly, constitutional laws
form a higher law because of their content. Ideally, a constitution will
express the fundamental principles and values that shape the political
structure and character of the state, thereby giving definite form and

direction to the state's government, its laws, and the larger society. How a constitution shapes the state's political *structure* is fairly straightforward. A constitution stipulates who governs, the extent of the government's authority, and what relation the people stand in to the government. A constitution should spell out how statutory laws are enacted, enforced, and applied. And a constitution may enumerate any individual or collective rights the state pledges to protect. How a constitution shapes the state's political *character* is somewhat subtler. To see how constitutional laws can both reflect and foster the fundamental character of a state, let us compare the constitutions of two contemporary states, Finland and the United States.

Section 19(1) of the Finnish Constitution reads,

> Those who cannot obtain the means necessary for a life of dignity have the right to receive indispensable subsistence and care.

Thus, in Finland, all people have a constitutional right to the basic material requirements for life, such as food, clothing, and housing. Those who cannot provide these necessities for themselves are guaranteed government assistance. The American Constitution contains no comparable provision. That is not to say the United States allows vast hordes of people starve. Various government agencies provide for those of lesser means, and charitable organizations catch most of those who fall through the official safety net. Nevertheless, the welfare reform of the late 1995 made it clear that a subsistence income is not a constitutionally guaranteed right in the United States. Under the new welfare legislation, people may receive welfare assistance for up to five years, but after that, they are cut off and must fend for themselves. Although this legislation had its detractors, most Americans agreed some such reform was needed, to break the cycle of dependence into which many welfare recipients had fallen. This reflects the fact that the United States, as a nation, is deeply committed to the ideal of individualism. Individual liberties are vigorously protected in America, but at the same time, individuals are accorded substantial responsibilities. Underlying this mindset is a genuine optimism concerning the potential of the individual: Americans believe that virtually anyone can succeed as long as they work hard enough and that the fulfillment one discovers in succeeding on one's own outweighs any hardships this may entail. Welfare reform was therefore promoted as a "tough love" measure most directly benefiting those who had become dependent on welfare—the deadlines were intended to spur recipients into action, so they could fulfill their potential as individuals.

In Finland, where the welfare system is more generous to begin with, there are likewise problems associated with welfare dependence. Nevertheless, reform legislation of the American variety never even enters mainstream political discussion, for such measures would patently violate both the Finnish Constitution and the Finnish psyche. The Finnish value system, like that of most European countries, places less emphasis on the individual and more on collective welfare and responsibility. Individuals still have their rights and responsibilities in the social welfare state. The Finns and most other Europeans collectively believe, however, that the state exists to promote the welfare of its members, such that it would not properly be a state if it allowed some people to fall through the cracks. In guaranteeing the material necessities of life, the Finnish Constitution both reflects and promotes this belief—the highest law of the land proclaims the society as a whole to be responsible for making sure everybody gets fed. Any welfare reform contemplated in Finland must therefore operate by some logic other than that of prodding welfare recipients into action by hanging the sword of an absolute cut-off date over them. Whether the Finnish or American approach to welfare is superior need not be debated here. It may simply be observed that the constitutions of both countries are appropriate in the provisions they include and do not include, for each reflects the general character of its society and helps to ensure that this character will endure over time.

A Strong Constitution

Given that a constitution forms a higher law that can shape the fundamental structure and character of a state, I take it as axiomatic that any state enacting a constitution has in interest in making its constitution as strong as possible. By "strong," I mean the constitution actually impresses a definite structure and character on the state, with visible effects on its institutions, its statutory laws, and the larger society. In a state with a strong constitution, government institutions will be organized according to a coherent set of principles, with the

diverse institutions all playing clearly defined roles in helping to realize the value system proclaimed by the constitution. The statutory
laws enacted will generally cohere with these values, both because of
specific legal constraints the constitution imposes and because lawmakers will typically share the constitution's broader values. Finally,
the government and the laws will enjoy a legitimacy in the eyes of the
people, who have themselves bought into this same set of values, and
who derive part of their identity from membership in the state. In a
state with a weak constitution, conversely, government institutions
will have no clear mission in terms of any coherent set of values.
Consequently, institutions will generally function, not in the interest
of the larger society, but on the principles of self-perpetuation and
self-aggrandizement. Similarly, with the mass of statutory laws having
no organizing theme, those laws enacted will tend to serve the interests of lawmakers and their benefactors. Finally, in a state with a weak
constitution, people will feel little ownership in their government,
nor will they gain any sort of identity from belonging to the state, the
state having no guiding principles into which the people could buy. No
state going to the trouble of enacting a constitution could desire to
engender such a fragmented, demoralizing atmosphere, so we may say
that any state that enacts a constitution has an interest in making its
constitution as strong as possible.

What makes a constitution strong? This question could likely be
given many answers, but I believe the most important characteristic
of a strong constitution is leanness. That is, a constitution should
contain only those laws that materially help define the structure and
character of the state; all other laws should be relegated to the sphere
of statutory law. The reasoning behind this claim is simple. Imagine a
constitution containing twenty articles, all of which pertain to either
the basic structure of the government or the rights and responsibilities
of individual citizens. Now imagine this same constitution with eighty
more articles added, dealing with matters ranging from military pen-
sions to traffic regulations to the penal code. How has this bulking up
the constitution actually weakened it? For one thing, the increase in
the sheer number of provisions diminishes the weight any one of
them can bear, attention now being divided among more provisions.
Moreover, mixing laws that concern everyday affairs in with truly
constitutional provisions drags the constitutional provisions down
from their exalted position, until they are accorded scarcely more re-

spect than statutory laws. Every state with cars on its roads must have a law determining which side of the road people are to drive on. But whether the left or right side is mandated does not affect the fundamental structure or character of the state. If a constitutional provision concerning free speech were to be followed by a provision mandating driving on the right side of the road, the free speech provision would suddenly seem much less weighty, both because attention had been split between it and the traffic provision and because its close proximity to a traffic regulation had deprived it of its gravity.

The above points are easy enough to grasp, but they may be driven home by borrowing an example from the Bible. Compare the Ten Commandments, presented to Moses in the book of Exodus, with the law code Moses receives in Leviticus. Although neither is a constitution *per se*, both were intended to provide the early Jewish people with rules by which to shape their social, moral, and spiritual lives. The Ten Commandments contain, of course, only ten provisions, and all are fairly basic in nature, prohibiting such anti-social acts as lying, stealing, adultering, and killing, while positively prescribing love for God and one another. This succinct set of laws has helped shape the western conscience for over 2500 years, and many Jews and Christians today still cite the Ten Commandments as forming the cornerstone of their moral thinking. The Levitican code, in contrast, contains hundreds of provisions that range from, "You shall eat no fat of ox, or sheep, or goat," to, "You shall not round off the hair on your temples or mar the edges of your beard."[2] This lengthy document provides a far more detailed guide to individual and collective conduct than does the Ten Commandments. As such, it must have been useful to Moses as he set about organizing the Jewish nation. Yet, who today other than a biblical scholar could cite a single provision of the Levitican code, beyond a passage frequently quoted to denounce homosexuality? No one today knows Leviticus, much less claims to make it the cornerstone of their moral thinking. As it happens, the Levitican code contains the same bans on lying, stealing, adultering, and killing as the Ten Commandments. This fact is lost on most Bible readers, however, for these prohibitions are buried among regulations concerning sacrifices, sanitation, and who may not see whom naked. Indeed, the bans on killing and stealing in Leviticus hardly seem that momentous, being placed on the same footing as dietary restrictions and health care regulations. The Bible specifically says the Levitican laws are the word of God, just like the Ten Commandments. But this more detailed code has not been able to maintain the aura of a higher law, given its preoccupation with such mundane matters as men's hairstyles.

Most of the Levitican laws are, in fact, properly statutory in nature, concerning issues quite specific to a particular people at a particular time. Statutory laws are not as exalted as constitutional laws, but they are just as necessary for the maintenance of the state. The Levitican ban on eating sheep fat, for instance, probably saved numerous lives in a time before people had learned to prepare meats safely. Still, such empirically based laws will be left out of a strong constitution to keep the constitution lean. Indeed, leaving properly statutory laws out of the constitution helps them to do their job better, since this type of law requires a flexibility that constitutional law lacks. As Edmund Randolph, one of the participants at the American Constitutional Convention, observed, a constitution should contain,

> essential principles only, lest the operations of government should be clogged by rendering these provisions permanent and unalterable which ought to be accommodated to times and events.[3]

Imagine the framers of the Constitution had drafted an article mandating that all public buildings have a hitching post out front—a law some municipalities did enact in statutory form. When cars then replaced horses as the standard means of transportation, rather than simply changing the law by statutory means, the nation would have had to go through the much more cumbersome process of constitutional amendment. This is certainly an inefficient means of updating relatively minor points of public policy. Moreover, locating properly statutory laws in the constitutional sphere can muddy political discourse by injecting questions of principle into debates that should concern empirical facts. Which side of the road cars drive on, for instance, should be decided on the basis of scientific studies investigating which arrangement will produce the safest and most efficient transportation network, not by invoking any abstract principles concerning the superiority of "leftness" or "rightness." Yet, constitutional debates are essentially debates about principles, so discussing properly statutory issues in a constitutional context will inevitably result in empirical data being skewed by peoples' beliefs about what *should* be the case, on principle. Finally, while an impassioned refusal to compromise on one's core principles may be admirable, this steadfastness can turn into a brutish intransigence in the statutory arena—an arena where compromise is a necessary democratic principle—when properly statutory and constitutional matters are jumbled together in a constitution.

Constitutionalism and the American Constitution

The framers of the American Constitution were certainly aware of the principle of leanness. The Constitution contains only seven articles, all of which deal almost exclusively with the structure of the federal government and its relation to the states. These few articles nevertheless manage to proclaim the fundamental principles and ideals that have guided the United States throughout its history and continue to guide it today. The overriding, unambiguous message of the American Constitution is, "We will not abide tyranny!" This is proclaimed, first of all, by the fact that the framers insisted on drafting a written constitution, as compared to the "unwritten" English Constitution. The English Constitution is an amalgamation of such legal documents as the Magna Carta and the English Bill of Rights, statutory laws, judicial interpretations, and customs. Although all these components of the Constitution have documentary support, no single document lays down exactly what laws the Constitution does and does not contain. Historically, this has given English governments a certain amount of latitude in determining what sort of governmental actions are constitutional. The American colonists regarded this as a major factor in the ability of the British government to tyrannize over them and deprive them of their rights as British subjects: the colonists had no written constitution to which they could refer to point out specifically how they were being wronged. Having won independence, therefore, the American framers resolved to enact a constitution as solid and publicly accessible as Hammurabi's Code. As in early Babylon, this would ensure that the law reign supreme in the United States, not the whims of any particular members of government.

Enacting a written constitution further ensured that the distinction between constitutional and statutory law would be drawn more sharply in the United States than in England. Indeed, probably no other country has granted its constitution such an exalted status as the United States: Americans treat their constitution as sacred writ and its framers as secular saints, while regarding any suggestion that its provisions be relaxed as blasphemous. This imprint the Constitution has left on American society is evidence of its strength. Much of this strength is no doubt due to the wisdom of the Constitution's specific provisions. The Constitution's leanness, however, has allowed these provisions to exert their full force in shaping the nation.

Actually, as originally drafted, the Constitution was so lean that calls for its amendment started going out even before it was ratified. Notably absent from the Constitution was any detailed enumeration of individual rights and liberties. Hence, the first Congress to meet under the Constitution drafted a bill of rights, ten amendments of which were ultimately ratified by the states. Included among these was the Second Amendment, guaranteeing a right to keep and bear arms. Why did the framers add this amendment to the Constitution? Why was a law invoking a right to bear arms viewed as something that would shape the structure and character of America, rather than being just another matter for statutory treatment? Developing a full answer to this question will require examining the history leading up to the drafting of the Bill of Rights. The next chapter begins this examination by looking back to America's English origins, tracing the development of the right to bear arms in the mother country.

CHAPTER 2

The Right to Bear Arms: English Origins

Unlike most of the other rights protected by the United States Constitution, the right to bear arms is almost wholly unique to the Anglo-American tradition. And while the English Bill of Rights of 1689 calls the right to bear arms an "ancient" and "undoubted" right, historian Joyce Lee Malcolm points out that, in fact, this right was first recognized in England in that same Bill of Rights.[1] Nor, glancing at English history, does the development of a constitutionally protected right to bear arms appear to have been inevitable. England's island geography, her historical resistance to absolutism, and her system of class privileges all played roles in the emergence of the English right to bear arms. But a strong dose of religious intolerance and two revolutions were also needed for the *duty* of bearing arms to be transformed, first into a *privilege* extended only to a few and only later into a constitutional *right*.

A Well-Armed Citizenry

From the time of the Norman invasion through the seventeenth century, owning a weapon was a duty in England. Every able-bodied man was required by law to be prepared to defend self, neighbor, and country, and this meant keeping and maintaining the appropriate arms as well as being proficient in their use. England did not have a professional police force until 1839, so deterring crime required having an armed citizenry capable of defending itself. The lack of police also made it necessary for people to come together to defend their communities. Thus, anyone witnessing an attack or crime was responsible for raising the "hue and cry," alerting one's neighbors to the trouble, then joining the sheriff in a search for the perpetrators. Men were also required to periodically perform "watch and ward" duty at the town gates, bringing their own weapons. A man could further be called to help the sheriff put down a riot as a member of the *posse comitatus*. Finally, every able-bodied male age sixteen to sixty was required to serve in the militia, reporting for musters with the appropriate weaponry. For a commoner, this meant bringing a long bow or pike and, later, a musket. A large landowner was typically required to equip a cavalryman with horse, arms, and armor.

In relying on a militia to defend the nation against foreign invasion and domestic insurgency, rather than a standing army, England bucked the trend of the continental powers. A standing army is a full-time, professional fighting force that remains together even during peacetime, constantly drilling when there is no real fighting to do. Both officers and soldiers typically make a career of the army, sometimes hiring themselves out as mercenaries to foreign princes. A militia, in contrast, is a part-time, unpaid army that comes together only when war or civil unrest appears immanent or for occasional drills. In the English militia, large landowners formed the militia's officer corps, with their tenants making up the rank and file. Both officers and soldiers were therefore mostly agricultural men. Militia service was something done on the side, and it was often seen as an onerous duty, in that it took men away from their primary vocations. The main reason England chose to rely on a militia was cost: maintaining a standing army was expensive, whereas mustering ordinary citizens only when needed and requiring them to bring their own weapons was relatively cheap. It was also believed that men defending their homes would fight more vigorously than professional soldiers simply doing a job. Indeed, the inevitable grumbles about militia service notwithstanding, it was hoped this duty would provide the average Englishman with a sense of pride and patriotism, knowing he was responsible for defending his nation.

Despite the advantages of a militia, England recognized that relying on the militia for national defense had some drawbacks. First, no matter how spirited a militia corps might be, a part-time army can never be as well trained and disciplined as a full-time, professional army. By the same token, a militia with a "bring your own arms" policy can never be as efficient as an army that supplies its troops with weapons, thereby standardizing its weaponry and ensuring that all weapons are of appropriate type and quality. Furthermore, if the militiaman may fight with great zeal when defending his homeland, he is likely to get dispirited when pulled away from his fields to fight in some distant place for a cause bearing no apparent relation to his interests. This more or less limits the usefulness of militias to defensive operations. These disadvantages inherent to any militia did cause some nervousness in England, especially when it was seen how badly continental countries that did not have standing armies suffered during the Thirty Years War. As an island country, however, England managed to stay out of most of the perpetual squabbles taking place on the continent, and her navy protected her against sudden attacks, so the English generally felt they could afford to rely on a militia during peacetime.

One other implication of England's reliance on the militia could be viewed as either an advantage or a disadvantage, depending on one's perspective. Specifically, putting the defense of the nation in the hands of the militia transferred a share of the king's "power of the sword" to Parliament and the gentry, on the one hand, and to the common people, on the other. England had always had a stronger parliamentary tradition than any of the continental powers. England was still a monarchy, and the English king enjoyed a large number of traditional prerogatives that allowed him to rule by decree on many issues. Moreover, as commander of the army, the king was able to enforce his decisions though the threat or actual use of force; hence his "power of the sword." To pass any laws, however, the king had to go through Parliament. And since Parliament determined how all national revenues would be spent, the king was dependent on Parliament for all his funding, including that of both his court and the army. Parliament was thus able to keep a check on royal authority by exercising its "power of the purse." The militia threw an additional factor into this dynamic. Any standing army was viewed as the king's army. Only Parliament could authorize funding of the army, but once assembled, the army, with its professional officer corps that reported directly to the king, could be assumed to be loyal to the king. The king also commanded the militia, and only he had the power to call it out. Yet, the field commanders in the militia were all local landowners, and they could interpret any orders from the king in the manner they best saw fit, energetically mustering their tenants, or responding very sluggishly. The king therefore depended on the good graces of the landowning gentry for any sort of effective use of the militia. This same gentry composed Parliament, so if the standing army was the king's army, the militia was more Parliament's force. Consequently, during those periods of English history when there was no standing army, or only a small one, yet most of the county's able-bodied males were ready to report for militia duty at short notice, reasonably well-armed and well-trained, Parliament was in a position to make significant demands of the king. Understandably, English kings often pressed Parliament to grant them larger standing armies, but both political and economic realities forced the crown to accept the institution of the militia.

It was not just Parliament and the gentry, however, that gained political clout through the militia. By composing the ranks of the militia, commoners also acquired a share in the "power of the sword." The mere fact that virtually every man in the country owned a military-style weapon, was trained to use it, and regularly drilled together with his neighbors meant that the people always retained at least the latent threat of revolt. Yet, even without going to the lengths of armed rebellion, commoners could use their country's dependence on the militia to exert political leverage. If the king called out the militia for a campaign that people felt bore no relation to their interests, they could always just stay home. Failing to report for musters was, of course, illegal, and it could be prosecuted. But if some of the men who did report to musters were sent out to round up the no-shows, this meant even fewer men were available for immediate service in the actual campaign. Another favorite means of subverting the king's military plans was to show up for musters unarmed or carrying one's oldest, rustiest weapon. This, too, bordered on criminality, but if hundreds of men reported for musters with no serviceable weapons, pleading poverty (when in fact many had good weapons buried under the barn floor), there was little the local commander or the king could do to turn the group into a fighting force. Hence, the king was always constrained to some degree in his military ventures, for he knew that if he were to get involved in a truly unpopular war, he might end up without any decent soldiers or weapons with which to fight.

Key Events: 1639–1671

One of the best examples of both gentry and commoners using "passive resistance" to militia service to frustrate the powers of the king came at the beginning of a series of events that would eventually transform the English duty to bear arms into a legal right. In 1639, Charles I launched an invasion of Scotland, intending to compel the Presbyterian Scots to adopt the Anglican Book of Common Prayer in their church services. A century previous, Henry VIII had broken with the Catholic Church and established the Church of England, with the English king at its head. The Anglican Church basically adopted Protestant theology, while retaining the high church rituals of the Catholic Church. Ever since that time, Anglicans had been oppressively intolerant of the English minority who remained Catholic, constantly charging that the "papists" were plotting to return England to Roman control. When Charles moved against Scotland, he did so in the name of Anglicanism. Charles, however, was widely suspected of having Catholic sympathies—his wife was Catholic—so his attempt to impose high church rituals on the Presbyterians was viewed as more of an attempt to catholicize this unthreatening branch of Protestantism than to anglicize it. The Scottish invasion was consequently highly unpopular in England. Landowners and tenants together conspired to avoid paying the taxes levied to support the campaign, and they reported for musters with only their least serviceable weapons. Some militiamen were conscripted into the regular army, but they frequently refused to submit to army obedience, and many deserted before the army reached Scotland. Left with no real army with which to advance, Charles was forced to arrange an embarrassing peace and to withdraw the offending prayer book.

Two years later, in 1641, another key event in the history of English gun policy took place: the Catholic minority in Ireland revolted, reportedly massacring 30,000 Protestants. The actual number of deaths turned out to be much lower, but the result was a wave of anti-Catholic hysteria sweeping through England and an attempt to disarm all Catholics. Ever since gun ownership had become wide-spread, both Parliament and the crown had realized that, in a well-armed county where subversion is feared by some particular group, the most effective way to rob the suspected group of its subversive power is by taking away its guns. Catholics were always regarded as the most subversive group in English society, so most early gun control meas-ures were directed against them. Previously, Catholics in many dis-tricts had been required to keep all guns not needed for self-defense at the municipal armory. This left them with access to the weapons they needed for militia service, while preventing them from stockpiling guns at home for any sort of insurrection. But it also left most Catholic families with at least one gun in the house for self-defense. The Irish massacre put an end to this leniency, and bands of Protes-tants went house to house through Catholic neighborhoods—often with no real authority—conducting searches, seizing weapons, and sometimes jailing Catholics or throwing them out of town.

The Irish Rebellion brought relations between Charles and the rabidly anti-Catholic Parliament close to a breaking point. Until the Scottish debacle, Charles had not even summoned Parliament for eleven years, scraping by on his personal income rather than solicit-ing funds from Parliament. In the wake of the Irish Rebellion, Parlia-ment issued a Grand Remonstrance cataloguing all of Charles's wrongs since his ascension to the throne, and demanding a series of reforms that would place strict constitutional limits on the crown. In early 1642, Parliament passed a Militia Bill that essentially shifted com-mand of the military from the king to Parliament. Parliament then took the unprecedented step of declaring the law effective, even if Charles did not sign it. When Charles refused to cede his military command, a struggle broke out for individual militia units and town armories. By late 1642, full-scale civil war had erupted between roy-alists and parliamentarians, with both sides mustering the militia in the areas under their control. Interestingly, both sides reported nu-merous men showing up for musters without any guns, although it is not clear whether they truly had none, they were protesting the fighting, or they feared having their guns confiscated for the war ef-fort. In any case, both sides quickly developed thriving arms indus-tries, and the country was soon flooded with guns. The fighting lasted until 1646, when Charles was forced to surrender to Scottish troops allied with Parliament. Refusing to negotiate with the parliamentary leadership, Charles was put on trial, and in 1649 was beheaded.

When Oliver Cromwell took control of the new republican government—which had a House of Commons, but no king or House of Lords—his most pressing domestic task was to restore order in a country torn apart by civil war. This was made difficult by the fact that large numbers of people owned guns, and tensions were still running high between parliamentarians and royalists. Cromwell knew he did not have the power to carry out a general disarmament, but selective disarmament had already been proven effective in its use against the Catholics. Cromwell's government therefore began dividing peopled into two classes, the "well-affected" and the "malignant." Of necessity, the vast majority of the population was deemed well-affected toward the new government, and these people were allowed to keep their guns. Malignants were those whom the government viewed as potential threats, including Catholics, staunch royalists, and dissenting Protestants. Such people were denied the privilege of owning guns and subjected to frequent searches and seizures, as well as other types of harassment, often by local militia units. Meanwhile, a standing army of as many as 40,000 soldiers was kept garrisoned about the country to maintain order.

Cromwell, ruling as "Lord Protector," was able to hold the country together for over a decade through the sheer force of his personality. When Cromwell died, however, Englishmen admitted they could not govern themselves without a monarch. The young Charles Stuart, who had been living in exile in France, was called back to England in 1660 and crowned Charles II. He was restored on the unspoken agreement that the crown would henceforth be subject to strict constitutional limits, and many members of Parliament no doubt believed that, as Charles's king-maker, they would be owed a certain deference. The "merry king" smilingly acquiesced and pledged to pardon most of his father's former enemies. Yet, he knew it was by ceding too much power to Parliament and the people that his father had lost control of the country. Hence, once restored, Charles quietly set out to secure a power more absolute than had been enjoyed by any of his English predecessors.

As had been the case for Cromwell, the first problem Charles faced on taking the throne was that his subjects owned far more weapons than he had at his command. A pair of minor uprisings early

in his rule gave him the excuse to retain a small army, which he re-
named "guards" in a public relations move designed to quell fears
about a standing army. Charles also revived the distinction between
"well-affected" and "malignants," and began disarming—and in some
cases jailing—his political opponents. No one questioned this disarmament policy in principle, but concerns began to arise that perhaps
Charles was being more vigorous in his disarmament of Protestants
than of Catholics. Nor were people mistaken in the suspicion that
Charles had personal leanings towards Catholicism, for his brother was
Catholic, and on his deathbed Charles sent away the Anglican priest in
favor of a Catholic one. Most importantly, in 1670 Charles signed a
secret agreement with Louis XIV of France, promising to make a public profession of his Catholic faith when the time was "convenient."
In exchange, Charles received a promise of troops to help enforce
Catholic rule in England and an annual allowance of £200,000. The
convenient moment apparently did not come until Charles's last, but
the deal gave him the money he needed to maintain his guards without
reliance on parliamentary funds. Thus, by 1671, Charles enjoyed the
relatively secure position of having disarmed most of his opponents,
while maintaining a small standing army completely under his control.

How was Parliament reacting to all of this? Most of the gentry
were intensely anti-Catholic, so they were troubled by the leniency
Charles was showing Catholics. Even more distressing was the fact
that Charles had no legitimate sons, thus leaving his Catholic brother,
James, heir to the throne. Parliament was moreover distrustful of
Charles's guards, and refused to grant Charles any parliamentary funds
to expand the corps. Nevertheless, everyone was tired of war, and
most of the gentry were preoccupied with restoring their own estates.
Parliament, moreover, was in complete control of the militia's purse
strings, and the gentry had reasserted itself as the militia's officer
corps, so the traditional balance between king and army, on the one
hand, and Parliament and militia, on the other, appeared to be holding
stable. Parliament seemed content to maintain the status quo.

Then, in 1671, Parliament did something completely unexpected.
With no fanfare and scarcely any opposition, Parliament passed a
Game Act that essentially forbade the private ownership of guns by all
non-gentry. Suddenly, the whole concept of the citizen militia had
been turned on its ear, since commoners could hardly be required to
report for musters bearing guns they were forbidden to own. What

could have led Parliament pass such an act, which apparently undercut one of its own primary sources of power? Addressing this question requires taking a look at the history of hunting and game legislation in England.

The Game Laws

The hunt had long been the cherished sport of the English nobility. Commoners might have valued wild game as a source of meat and skins, but the gentry loved hunting simply for the thrill of the sport. And with a limited amount of forest acreage in the country, there was no question about who would be given preference for hunting it. Huge wilderness parks were therefore set aside for hunting, many being fenced in to ensure that the game remained in place. The king owned some of these game parks; other great nobles owned others. For the commoner living near a game park, it must have been tempting to sneak in and shoot a deer or snare a rabbit. Since 1389, however, a series of Game Acts had been passed to combat poaching, and thus protect sport hunting. In one form or another, all these acts established property qualifications for the use of dogs, nets, snares, guns, or other "engines of the hunt" for purposes of hunting. This ensured that only the landowning elite could legally hunt. Still, commoners had not traditionally been barred from *owning* engines of the hunt; such equipment had only become illegal when a commoner actually used it for hunting. This changed in 1671.

One of the hardest-hit victims of the English Civil War had been the game park. When war broke out and the forest wardens were called away from their duties, commoners living near the game parks began wreaking havoc on them. Not only were trees cut down for firewood and game hunted for food and profit, but some game seems to have been slaughtered simply as an expression of anger directed against the royal and gentrified forces that had originally fenced off the parks. By the time Charles II was restored, the game parks were filled with squatters, the fences enclosing many had been torn down, and some parks were completely devoid of game. An avid hunter, Charles made restoration of the game parks one of his top priorities, to the point of importing deer from Germany to restock some of the royal forests. The gentry probably would have supported Charles in

these efforts purely out of love of the hunt. But the gentry had suffered as a class nearly as badly as the game parks during the Civil War
and interregnum. The separation between gentry and commoner had
been diminished as men fought side by side in the war. Living for ten
years without a king—the head of the old feudal system that ultimately gave the gentry their class prerogatives—further eroded the
class distinction. Finally, a class of non-landed, wealthy, urban indus-
trialists was beginning to emerge and challenge the preeminence of
the rural gentry. Hence, beyond longing for the thrill of the chase, the
gentry felt it had to reestablish its class prerogatives, and reaffirming
its exclusive right to hunt was one of the ways it could do this. Accordingly, Parliament decided it had a greater interest in working with
Charles to reestablish the hunt than in actively opposing his gradual
drift towards absolutism, and it passed the unprecedentedly restrictive
Game Act of 1671. Commoners were thereby deprived of their longstanding privilege of bearing arms, not by the king, but by their traditional partner in checking royal power by means of their private
arms, Parliament.

Perhaps what is most remarkable about the Game Act of 1671 is
the ease with which it sailed through Parliament, clearing both houses
and gaining the king's assent in slightly more than a month, with little recorded debate. This may indicate that many members of Parliament viewed the Game Act purely as a hunting bill, without stopping
to consider the political ramifications of disarming the vast majority
of the population. More likely, however, Parliament passed the Game
Act precisely because the gentry had begun to appreciate the implications of placing a gun in the hands of every commoner. After the
general mobilization of the Civil War, no one could ignore the fact
that an armed populace would always be capable of using its guns, not
just to resist royal authority under the command of the gentry, but
also to challenge the authority of this same gentry. Accordingly, the
enforcement clause of the Game Act empowered landlords to send
gamekeepers to search for and seize weapons from their tenants. Of-
fenders were then to be tried before a single justice of the peace. Since
most landlords were justices, this effectively gave landowners the
power to disarm any of their tenants they saw fit. This arrangement
facilitated the crackdown on poaching, while allowing the gentry to
disarm such threatening groups as Catholics, with whom Charles was
being so lenient. And far from rendering the militia obsolete, it actu-

ally strengthened the militia as a tool of parliamentary power, since the gentry could leave its own supporters in possession of guns, while disarming any commoners sympathetic to the king. Indeed, the Game Act was never broadly enforced; no large-scale disarmaments are reported. The ban on gun ownership by commoners rather gave the gentry the power to selectively disarm whomever it chose, whether poacher, Catholic, royalist, or potential rebel of any other stripe.

The English Bill of Rights

When Charles died in 1685, he was succeeded on the throne by his Catholic brother, crowned James II. Parliament was apprehensive but appears to have been willing to wait out a period of Catholic rule, especially since James had no sons, and his wife appeared to be past her childbearing years. James, however, believed he would have to establish an absolute monarchy on the model of his cousin and hero, Louis XIV, if he wanted to remain in power. To this end, he began disarming his political opponents—mostly Protestant—even more vigorously than had his brother. Some disarmed Catholics even got their guns back. At the same time, James relieved numerous Protestant army and navy officers of their commands and replaced them with Catholics. Then, when the militia proved ineffective in putting down an uprising against him, James doubled the size of the standing army. All of these measures should have put James in a secure position, at least militarily. The antipathy he managed to generate, however, due to both his heavy-handedness and his Catholicism, left him with no popular base of support. Consequently, when James's wife unexpectedly gave birth to a son, thereby giving James a male Catholic heir, Parliament appealed to James's Protestant son-in-law, William of Orange, to come and claim the throne. William landed in England in 1689, and James fled to France without a fight. The "Glorious Revolution" had been carried out with scarcely a drop of blood shed.

This time, when Parliament put a king on the throne, it was not going to do so merely hoping the new monarch would observe constitutional limits. It was going to make this demand at the outset and get the agreement in written form. William accepted the political reality of the situation, and, before ascending to the throne, convened a parliamentary convention to draft a "new magna carta" that would spell out the constitutional limits to which the crown would henceforth be subject. The convention produced the Declaration of Rights, later put into statutory form as the Bill of Rights, which listed thirteen grievous wrongs committed by James, followed by a positive formulation of the thirteen corresponding rights or laws he had violated. While the Declaration labels these rights "true, ancient, and indubitable," at least eight of its thirteen articles broke new legal ground.[2] In many cases, Parliament simply used the Declaration as an opportunity to codify rights or monarchical limits that for years it had merely wished kings would observe. William did not actually sign the Declaration of Rights, but it was read aloud at his coronation, and he verbally acknowledged it before accepting the crown.

The two articles the Bill of Rights that concern us here are Articles 5 and 6. The negative clause of Article 5 complains that James acted illegally

> By raising and keeping a standing army within this kingdom in time of peace without consent of Parliament and quartering soldiers contrary to law.

The corresponding positive clause asserts

> That the raising or keeping a standing army within the kingdom in time of peace, unless it be with consent of Parliament, is against law.

In theory, Parliament had always controlled the existence, size, and mission of the army through its power of the purse. In fact, because the king could always find ways of circumventing funding limits, standing armies during peacetime had long been a source of contention between Parliament and the crown. Parliament itself had ceded some of its authority when it allowed Charles II to maintain a standing army of any size, providing he paid for it himself; no one foresaw the secret treaty with Louis XIV. So by the time England overthrew its second king bent on achieving more absolute power by means of a larger standing army, Parliament was ready to eliminate any ambiguity concerning who controlled the status of the army. Hence, Article 5 gives Parliament the authority to eliminate the army during peacetime, whatever its source of funding. Indeed, Article 5 strongly suggests the standard practice in England would be to have no standing army during peacetime. The corollary is that the militia would once again be given primary responsibility for defending England. Not only would this be cheaper than maintaining a standing army, but it would give Parliament the muscle it needed to ensure that William and all future monarchs adhere to the constitutional limits laid out in the Bill of Rights and elsewhere.

Article 6 charges that James acted illegally

> By causing several good subjects, being Protestants, to be disarmed at the same time when Papists were both armed and employed contrary to law.

The positive right prescribed is

> That the subjects which are Protestants may have arms for their defense suitable to their condition and as allowed by law.

Article 6 is striking both for how much it accomplishes and how little. On the one hand, it elevates something that had for hundreds of years been a duty, then a privilege, to the status of constitutional right. On the other hand, the Article attaches so many qualifications to the right to bear arms that it does not appear to have changed the laws or policies of England in any way. Most conspicuously, the right to bear arms is extended only to Protestants. Catholics and other non-Protestants still being considered too dangerous to be entrusted with weapons, Article 6 upholds the decades-old policy of allowing the well-affected to bear arms, while disarming malignants. Article 6 further limits its protection to arms which Protestants keep "for their defense." This explicitly denies constitutional protection for gun ownership for purposes other than defense, notably hunting. Indeed, the phrase "as allowed by law" makes clear that the right to bear arms would not be absolute, but could be abridged by any laws Parliament saw fit to pass. Finally, when the House of Lords added the phrase "suitable to their condition" to Article 6, these representatives of the great nobility were bluntly stating that gun laws could, nay, should discriminate on the basis of "condition," or socio-economic class. Yet, when the Bill of Rights was enacted in 1689, England already had a class-based gun law on the books: the Game Act of 1671, which established a property qualification for gun ownership. The Game Act allowed people of appropriate condition—large landowners—to possess firearms, so it was fully in compliance with Article 6. Consequently, Article 6 did *not* overturn the Game Act, and thus it did *not* extend a

right to bear arms to the vast majority of the English population.
That Parliament fully intended for the scope of Article 6 to be limited in this way is evidenced by the fact that an amendment to the
Article was proposed four years later that would have allowed every
Protestant, regardless of class, to keep one musket. The amendment
was voted down decisively, after a speech warning that it "savours of
the politics to arm the mob, which…is not very safe for any government."[3]

The English Right to Bear Arms

In the final analysis, therefore, the English right to bear arms, as conferred by the Bill of Rights of 1689, was not as a populist right but a
right created by and for an elite minority, the gentry, as represented
by Parliament. In drafting Articles 5 and 6 of the Bill of Rights, Parliament was erecting defenses on two fronts. On one front was the
crown. The gentry had long known a standing army would generally
be loyal to the king, whereas Parliament could count on the support
of the militia, the gentry composing its officer corps. And recent history had confirmed that monarchs will tend to usurp power from Parliament, if not checked. Thus, in order to limit the relative power of
the king, Parliament needed to control the king's ability to assemble
and maintain a standing army, while strengthening the institution of
the militia. A strong militia required that landowners always be armed,
and that they retain at least the option of arming their tenants, the
militia's foot soldiers. Massing on Parliament's second front, however, were these same tenants. The widespread availability of firearms
had left commoners more potentially dangerous than ever before, and
they had already shown their willingness to use violence to protect
their interests, for instance, when the re-enclosure of the game parks
triggered several riots. Meanwhile, the rise of urban industry had
spawned a growing class of poor laborers who bore no allegiance to
the landed gentry and thus who certainly could not be trusted with
guns. Hence, the gentry needed to be able to regulate gun ownership
by commoners, even as it used its tenants and their guns as a check on
royal power. Selective enforcement of the Game Act of 1671 gave
the gentry the flexibility it needed to juggle these competing demands,
and Article 6 of the Bill of Rights, far from extending a universal

right to bear arms, essentially sanctioned the gentry's policy of selective gun control.

Over the next hundred years, the right to bear arms in England was gradually extended to cover nearly all Protestants. Yet, perhaps because this right was originally designed to promote the interests of a very restricted class, it never became ingrained in the English psyche as a fundamental right. Consequently, when rising violent crime in the early twentieth century spurred the passage of several strict gun control bills, the right to bear arms essentially slipped out of the unwritten English Constitution, with little notice. Today, many English people find puzzling the American insistence on the sanctity of the right to bear arms. We need not concern ourselves with these later developments in England, however, for the historical backdrop against which the American colonists, and later the framers of the Constitution, would consider the right to bear arms has been established. Before turning to see what use a young country with no king and no gentry would make of a right with essentially aristocratic origins, however, we must examine some developments that took place in English political science contemporaneous to the political events we have been surveying.

CHAPTER 3

The Social Contract and Natural Rights

The seventeenth century was a time of great advances in the sciences, including the newly emerging field of political science. This science was born as thinkers took the traditional topics of political philosophy and applied new methods of scientific analysis to them. Several key concepts were either developed in the course of these analyses or given a new formulation. Two that would heavily influence the framers of the American Constitution were the concepts of the social contract and natural right. Properly interpreting the Second Amendment, in particular, depends on an understanding of these two concepts, so this chapter will trace their development in the works of the two most important English political scientists of the seventeenth century, Thomas Hobbes and John Locke.

Pre-Hobbesian Doctrine: The Divine Right of Kings

The question that drove seventeenth-century political science, both in England and on the continent, was, "Whence derives the sovereign its legitimacy?" And since all the larger European states were monarchies, the question became, "Whence derives the king his legitimacy?" The answer inherited from the Middle Ages was the doctrine of the divine right of kings. In a celebrated account of this doctrine, Sir Robert Filmer argued that God gave Adam sovereignty over all the earth. Since then, certain of Adam's descendents have inherited this sovereignty over various parts of the world, according to the laws of inheritance. Temporal kings therefore receive their authority from the one eternal king, whose right to govern is unquestioned. Charles I was a firm believer in divine right doctrine, and invoked it to justify his campaign to secure a more absolute power. Most of his subjects likewise accepted as a matter of course that kings were divinely appointed. This magnified their distress when Charles was executed: if the king was God's representative on earth, had the English not committed an act approaching a second crucifixion by killing him? Yet, England suffered no obvious divine retribution during the interregnum. As a result, divine right doctrine survived Charles's beheading little better than did Charles. After all, if God was going to allow a king to die without punishing his executioners, could the king have been so dear to God in the first place?

Hobbes and the Social Contract

As a supporter of the monarchy, Thomas Hobbes fled to Paris early in the English Civil War. Hobbes was no darling of the royalists, however, for though the classic work he wrote while in Paris, *Leviathan*, advocates an absolute monarchy, it overturns divine right as the basis of monarchic authority. Hobbes was the first in a line of great thinkers to propound what would become the accepted justification for sovereign power throughout western society: the social contract.

Impressed with the work of Galileo and other modern scientists, Hobbes proposed to apply the methods of scientific analysis to the study of politics. To this end, he maintained that, just as we study the workings of a watch by taking it apart and examining its individual components, we can best understand the workings of the state by considering how individual people would behave if all the laws, customs, and other restraints of civil society were taken away. Free from the trappings of civil society, people would occupy a "state of nature," where everyone acted according to their natural appetites and aversions, with the universal, overriding human drive being to preserve oneself. No laws govern the state of nature other than the law of force; one's freedom is limited only by the limits of one's powers. Thus, if I am hungry and see someone else with food, I may rip it from the other person's hands, provided I believe I am strong enough to do so without suffering a worse counterattack. This arrangement might appear to be advantageous to the strong, but in the state of nature, everyone will tend to be roughly equal in strength and intelligence. Consequently, no one will be immune to attack, and everyone will live in a constant state of fear and violence. As Hobbes writes, the state of nature is "such a warre, as is of every man, against every man,"[1] and human life in the state of nature must be "solitary, poore, nasty, brutish, and short."[2]

Weary of living in constant fear, at some point people must come together and strike up an agreement. Everyone agrees to give up certain of the freedoms they enjoy in the state of nature—including, most importantly, the freedom to injure one another—on the condition that everyone else makes the same concession. In return for this loss of freedom, everyone gains the security of living in a society ruled by law, rather than force. This agreement is the social contract.

The social contract would be meaningless, however, if not enforced. As Hobbes writes, "Covenants, without the Sword, are but Words, and of no strength to secure a man at all."[3] That is, if compliance with the society contract were merely voluntary, presumably I would respect the law only when it was in my best interest to do so. If I thought I could gain something by breaking the law, and I did not fear anyone injuring me in return, I would have every reason to ignore my earlier pledge to abide by the law. But in this case I act no differently than I did in the state of nature. And since I know everyone else must reason as I do, I enjoy no more security than I did in the state of nature. Hence, when people enter into the social contract, they must appoint a sovereign and accord him the power to enforce the laws of the state. Indeed, the sovereign must be granted absolute power, or the state would not be a civil society in the full sense. If the laws were only partially enforced, subjects would still calculate when it was in their best interest to follow the law and when to break it. Yet, this scarcely distinguishes civil society from the state of nature, where all decisions are made on the basis of such power calculations. Only when the sovereign has an absolute power to enforce the law do such calculations become pointless, since then lawbreaking can never be in anyone's best interest. And only when is the state is fully ruled by law does it truly constitute a civil society. Thus, the sovereign must be given even the power of life and death over his subjects. But this authority is legitimate, for his subjects invest him with it of their own free consent, in the interest of escaping from the violence and fear that characterized the state of nature.

Actually, while Hobbes stresses the need for an absolute sovereign, he concedes that no mundane ruler can possess truly absolute powers. This is because, though people can give up many of the freedoms they enjoy in the state of nature, there are certain rights people can never be deprived of, or even give up of their own free consent. Notably, the right to defend one's life can never be coherently forfeited. This is because any contract by which a person agreed to give up this right would be unenforceable; it would therefore be invalid, a meaningless "Covenant without the Sword." When I enter into a normal business contract, it makes sense for the other party to accept certain promises I make, for he knows my compliance with our contract can be enforced. If he sells me ten rifles for $1000, for instance, payment being due sixty days after delivery, he knows he can take me to court and collect damages exceeding $1000 should I fail to make payment. By the same token, I know I can sue him if the rifles turn out to be defective. Our contract is therefore perfectly coherent and valid, for it is enforceable on both sides. But assume that, in the state of nature, I sign a contract whereby I agree to forfeit my life, should I fail pay for the rifles within sixty days. When I do fail to make payment, my fellow contractant puts me in shackles, and begins making preparations for my execution. Terrified, I begin to struggle, and make every effort to escape. He says, "Come now, stop struggling. You freely consented to forfeit your life if you should fail to make payment. Now that you have done so, you have no right to resist death. You are, after all, bound by contract." To which I reply, "Forget the contract! I want to live!" And I continue to struggle. If my fellow contractant has used strong enough shackles, my resistance will do little good; he will kill me. But he can only do so over my resistance. This means I have not observed my side of the bargain—I have not freely submitted to death. Nor is there anything my fellow contractant can do to make me live up to my agreement, for to make me stop struggling, the worst he can do is threaten me with is death. But it is against death that I struggle, so his threats have no effect on me; I continue to fight. Hence, the contract we originally signed was never enforceable. An unenforceable contract being incoherent, it was invalid from the beginning.

When I agree to the larger social contract, I grant the sovereign the authority to kill me, should I break the law. But, Hobbes notes, I cannot coherently cede my right to resist when the sovereign actually sends his executioners after me. For even if I should pledge to give up the right to defend myself, the sovereign cannot hold me to this pledge: when I do try to defend myself, the sovereign can threaten me with nothing worse than death, and this threat has no power to make me stop struggling, since it is against death that I already struggle. Given that people cannot coherently give up their right to resist death, Hobbes concludes that when they draw up the social contract, they must grant the sovereign as much real, physical power as possible—they must accord him the strongest shackles possible. This reduces the chances of anyone *successfully* resisting the sovereign's rule essentially to zero. And only in this case will people obey the law virtually without exception, thus allowing everyone to enjoy the security of living in a truly civil society.

One important implication of Hobbes's account of the social contract is that revolt against a monarch can never be justified. When we enter into the social contract, then for better or for worse, we cede all authority to the sovereign. Acting in opposition to the king is therefore tantamount to reneging on the social contract. And Hobbes thought no rational person could ever want to do this, since living in a peaceful society, no matter how oppressive, will always be preferable to enduring the horrors of war; Hobbes believed the Civil War was demonstrating this even as he wrote *Leviathan*. Still, once Charles I had been executed, Hobbes made his peace with the interregnum government and returned to England, reasoning that revolt against Cromwell—who had established himself as the recognized leader of England—would be no more justified than the revolt against Charles had been. Hobbes welcomed the restoration of Charles II, whom he had tutored in mathematics in Paris. But Hobbes was never completely embraced by his former pupil. His support for absolute monarchy notwithstanding, the royalist camp believed—correctly—that Hobbes had undercut the crown's power by locating the grounds for its legitimacy, not in divine sanction, but in the free consent of the citizenry.

Yet, neither did the parliamentarians like Hobbes, for they could not stomach his assertion that civil society requires an absolute monarch. Indeed, even members of the gentry who had fought on Charles's behalf believed royal power should have some limits. The most widely perceived flaw in Hobbes's theory was that, while Hobbes correctly notes that contracts must be enforceable to be meaningful, he provides no means of enforcing the rule of law on the sovereign. Signatories of the Hobbesian social contract must simply trust that the person granted absolute power will use this power for the common good, not personal gain. Yet, as Lord Acton would later observe: "Power tends to corrupt and absolute power corrupts absolutely." Hobbes's only response was to argue that, if the sovereign can be subject to no earthly authority, he is answerable to the divine king, whose power is truly absolute. Thus, while Hobbes did not revert to divine right doctrine, he did find it necessary to invoke God to make his own theory work: the king derives his legitimacy from the consent of the people, but once invested with power, he is constrained to exercise it justly only by his fear of God. By the late 1680's, however, Englishmen had little faith in piety alone keeping a king honest. This helps explain why they embraced the version of contract theory put forth by an English philosopher a generation younger than Hobbes, John Locke.

Locke: Natural Law and Natural Right

Locke completed his most important political work, the *Second Treatise of Government*, a few months after William of Orange had been offered the English throne, and he dedicated his book to the new monarch. Like Hobbes, Locke begins his discussion of political legitimacy with an account of the state of nature. The Lockean state of nature is not as bleak as that of Hobbes, however, for Locke denies that the natural human condition is to be at war with one another. In fact, Locke explicitly distinguishes the state of nature from the state of war. In a state of war, no laws are observed beyond the law of force, and participants have a declared hostility to one another. Hobbes believed people to be so self-interested that, absent an absolute sovereign over them, they will necessarily be at war with one another. Locke replies that precisely *because* people are self-interested, the state of nature will not be characterized by warfare. Far from constantly attacking one another, people will tend to leave one another alone or even band together in informal communities on the reasoning that this will reduce the risk of suffering attacks or counterattacks.

Locke goes farther, however, and argues that people are bound by a natural law, and they enjoy certain natural rights in the state of nature. The natural law has two provisions. The first is that "no one ought to harm another in his life, health, liberty, or possessions." Indeed, a person ought, "as much as he can, to preserve the rest of mankind."[4] The second provision is that, if anyone should violate the first, then anyone else—and not just the victim—is entitled to exact retribution on the offender. Thus, if someone should steal a loaf of bread from my neighbor, my neighbor may rightfully track him down and punish him. But I am entitled to do the same, merely having witnessed a violation of natural law, even though I suffered no injury myself.

What is the origin of the natural law? What *is* the natural law, metaphysically speaking? Locke, unfortunately, is not absolutely clear on this point. Sometimes he makes the natural law sound like a divine law; other times it appears to have fully human origins. While the following account of natural law is certainly not the last word in Locke scholarship, I believe it squares best with the philosophy of empiricism, the school of thought Locke helped to found in his nonpolitical writings. According to empiricism, all human knowledge comes from experience, that is, from observation of the material world around us. Human reasoning is the power of making generalizations from experience. Based on their daily experiences, primitive people must have come to formulate such general laws of nature as, "The sun rises every morning." In the same way, people must learn from experience that if you attempt to kill or enslave other people, or you steal the material goods to which they have laid claim, this invites retaliation. Hence, just as people in the state of nature will come to formulate such prudential rules as, "Do not eat sheep fat, since it will make you sick," people will start making it a general rule not to harm others in their "life, health, liberty, or possessions," since this usually leads to more trouble than it is worth. People will further learn from experience that acts violating this rule tend to cause discord in the loose communities that spring up: harmony is replaced with violence and reprisal. And even in the state of nature, people will grasp that living in a stable community is preferable to isolation or warfare, so they will realize everyone has an interest in promoting compliance with the natural law. Hence, people will make it a general rule to exact retribution on violators of the natural law, no matter who the victim happens to be, both to punish the offender for threatening the community, and to deter future offenses. It is with the invocation of this "right of retribution" that a general rule which began as a purely prudential rule of thumb starts taking on the character of a moral law. As people reflect on the actions of themselves and others, they start judging these actions as being good or bad, and hence as meriting reward or punishment, based on their conformity to the natural law.

Beyond maintaining that people will observe a natural law even before entering civil society, Locke asserts that people have certain natural rights in the state of nature. Locke most often speaks of the natural right to one's "property," although he uses this term to refer, not just to material possessions, but also to one's life and liberty. In one sense, natural rights simply form the flip side of the natural law: according to natural law, I may not kill, enslave, or steal from others indiscriminately, so when I observe the natural law, I recognize others as having a right to life, liberty, and private property. This undoubtedly captures an important aspect of natural right. Still, Locke seems to mean something more when he uses this term. Indeed, whereas Hobbes often suggests that people have a right to do anything they want in the state of nature, within the limits of their power, when Locke uses the term "right," he generally restricts his meaning to those rights which no one can deprive a person of and which cannot coherently be given up even through a free act of will. For the sake of clarity, in this exposition the term "natural right" will henceforth designate such inalienable rights, with "natural freedom" referring to those freedoms we enjoy in the state of nature, but which we may coherently forfeit on entering civil society.

Why are the rights to life, liberty, and private property inalienable? Hobbes had already shown why no one can take away my right to defend my life: to make me stop defending myself, the worst another person can do is threaten me with death, and this threat carries no weight, since death is what I struggle against already. Nor may I coherently contract away this right, since I can only be held to my side of the bargain through the threat of death, and this threat does not sway me when my life already in jeopardy. Locke extends this argument to show that the right to defend one's liberty is an inalienable, natural right. When I am enslaved, my life is in my master's hands; should he decide to kill me, I lack the physical power to resist. Yet, I have an inalienable right to defend my life, so I likewise have a natural right to use whatever force I can muster to avoid enslavement, or to free myself from this condition, once enslaved. This means I cannot coherently contract away my liberty, even through a free act of will: not being able to coherently forfeit my right to self-defense, I cannot coherently put myself in a position where I have no physical possibility of defending myself. Thus, even if I should sign a contract selling myself into slavery, I am not bound by it. For once enslaved, I find myself in a condition where my life is threatened by the absolute power my master has over me. And since my master can threaten me with nothing worse than death, he cannot compel me to abide by my renunciation of freedom. Granted, my master can forestall any attempts at revolt through the threat of immediate death or through torture. But he can do nothing to prevent me from biding my time and attempting to free myself when the moment is favorable. Hence, I have not actually accepted my enslavement, nor can my master do anything to make me accept this condition, as opposed to simply bearing it for a time. My original commitment to give up all claim to liberty was therefore unenforceable, so the contract I signed was invalid, a meaningless covenant without possible sword.

This same argument may be extended to justify the natural right to claim possession of material goods. As human beings, we depend on a steady supply of material objects for our livelihood. Such goods can be found in nature, but they are of little use to humans until we somehow modify them through our labor—plucking the apple off its tree, if nothing else. Although there are no written property laws in the state of nature, when I modify a natural object through my labor, I essentially taken possession of it: I signal to others that it is mine, and that I intend to use it for my upkeep. Were I unable to take possession of material goods and consume them as I saw fit, I would quickly die of starvation or exposure. Assume, however, some powerful person tells me I may no longer appropriate goods for myself but may only eat when he deigns to feed me. My life is in constant jeopardy, being dependent on the other's whims. If the other person is powerful enough, he can force this arrangement on me. But he can

never force me to willfully accept my condition. I always retain my
right to resist this form of slavery, for no one can take away my right
to defend my life, so neither can anyone take away my right to appropriate and consume those goods necessary for my survival. Indeed,
I cannot even freely give up my right to hold possessions, for this
would equate to selling myself into slavery: I would lose the power to
ensure the conditions of my survival. That is not to say I cannot coherently give up certain of my possessions. I may very well trade
some goods I hold for others or even give away some possessions out
of sheer good will. I may further agree not to take possession of a certain type of object, assuming such objects are not necessary for my
survival. But I cannot coherently pledge to give up my right to take
possession of objects outright, for I could only be held to this pledge
through the threat of death, and this threat will be empty if I already
stand on the brink of starvation.

Hence, though no written laws or authorized sovereigns govern
the state of nature, people in the natural state will tend to observe a
natural law and to recognize certain natural rights of their own accord.
As a result, the state of nature will generally be far more peaceful than
Hobbes believed. Nevertheless, even the Lockean state of nature must
contain a good deal of violence and fear. For one thing, if all reasonable inhabitants of the state of nature will grasp that abiding by the
natural law is in one's own best interest, there is no guarantee everyone will be reasonable. And if one person manages to become much
stronger than others, it will probably be in that person's best interest
to exploit his neighbors. Thus, violations of the natural law will inevitably occur in the state of nature. And when attempts are made to
uphold the natural law through retribution, further conflicts will arise.
For though anyone may punish a violator of natural law, in most
cases it will be the victim, or someone close to the victim, who takes
action. This means someone with a vested interest in the case is responsible for deciding exactly what provisions of the natural law have
been broken, who did it, and what punishment the violator should suffer; this same person then carries out the punishment. In other words,
a single person serves as legislator, judge, and enforcer of the law,
moreover doing so in a case in which the person has a strong personal
interest and emotional bias. Not even the most reasonable and well-
meaning person can judge fairly under such circumstances, so punishments meted out in the state of nature will frequently contradict the

natural law just as egregiously as the original offenses. In sum, then, if the rule of law in the state of nature is real, it cannot be very strict, given than it depends for its enforcement primarily on the power of victims to retaliate. And because justice in the state of nature is essentially vigilante justice, it will be accompanied by all irregularities and biases thereof.

Locke and the Social Contract

Hence, as Hobbes argued, there must come a time when violence and fear drive the inhabitants of the state of nature to form a compact with one another and enter into civil society. So doing, each agrees to give up certain freedoms enjoyed in the state of nature and to submit to the formal rule of law in exchange for both security and civilly conferred rights. For Locke, those freedoms relinquished primarily relate to actions that violate the natural law, anyway, and hence would have been unlawful even in the state of nature. But whereas in the state of nature, individuals must enforce the natural law themselves, the sovereign is now vested, by common consent, with the power of making and enforcing laws. Indeed, the one right people enjoy in the state of nature which they must yield on entering civil society—not giving it up completely, but transferring it to the state—is the right of exacting retribution on violators of the law. If someone attacks me in civil society, I may still defend myself, the right to self-defense being inalienable. But if I survive the attack and my assailant escapes, I may not hunt him down and punish him myself. I must rather leave it to the designated authorities to apprehend the offender, judge him according to the established laws, and mete out any punishments deemed appropriate. Perhaps this retribution will not be as harsh as what I would have exacted. But I am biased, having been the victim of the attack, and it is precisely to escape the uncertainty and prejudice inherent to vigilante justice that we all agree to turn law enforcement over to the state.

If entering civil society entails giving up certain natural freedoms, as well as transferring the right of retribution to the state, Locke stresses that people cannot relinquish their natural rights to life, liberty, or possessions through the social contract, these rights being inalienable. He concludes that while the social contract must invest the sovereign with enough power to make and enforce laws, it cannot grant any person or group absolute power. To do so would effectively place the life, liberty, and possessions of every other member of society in the hands of the absolute ruler. But no one may coherently contract away the inalienable right to one's essential "property," so even if a social contract were signed that instituted an absolute ruler, it would be invalid, as incoherent. Thus, whereas Hobbes believed an absolute ruler to be necessary to civil society, Locke establishes that absolute authority can never be legitimate.

If civil society requires a sovereign, but the sovereign cannot be absolute, the biggest challenge any people founding a state must face is structuring the sovereign authority such that it may govern effectively, without becoming absolutistic. Locke's primary strategy for accomplishing this relies on a principle already institutionalized in the English political system: the separation of powers. As noted earlier, the main problem with the administration of justice in the state of nature is that the same person often serves as legislator, judge, and executive, moreover doing so in cases in which the person has a personal interest. An absolute ruler ultimately serves as legislator, judge, and executive in every case to arise among his subjects. And since the absolute ruler lays ultimate claim to all the property in the state, he has a personal interest in all the cases on which he rules. To remedy this situation, Locke suggests that the government be divided into three separate bodies invested, respectively, with legislative, executive, and federative powers. The legislative body is the supreme governing power in the state, for it makes the laws. The executive is then charged with enforcing these laws. By "federative" powers, Locke means the authority to deal with foreign states. He acknowledges that executive and federative powers will often be located in the same person, the head of state. But this is not problematic, since carrying out both domestic and foreign policy rarely leads to a conflict of interest. Locke even approves of the executive playing some role in the legislature, fully sanctioning the English system of mixed government, under which the crown is responsible for convening and dissolving Parliament, and may introduce bills. Locke stresses, however, that the executive cannot *be* the legislature. The bulk of legislative powers must reside in some person or group distinct from the person functioning as chief executive, to prevent the executive from passing laws directed more toward personal gain than the good of the state. Locke does not include the judiciary as one of the three primary branches of government, but he does insist on an independent judiciary, to ensure that neither lawmakers nor the executive can exempt themselves from the laws they establish and enforce. When a government is set up according to some such plan, different people make, enforce, and interpret the laws. This allows for effective governance, while preventing any one person or group from accumulating absolute power over the rest.

One important theoretical advance Locke makes over Hobbes is the introduction of his doctrine of tacit consent. An inevitable objection to Hobbesian contract theory is that *I* was not there for the signing of the social contract; *I* never gave my consent to being ruled. Why, then, should I be subject to the sovereign's authority? Locke grants that few of us were around when civil society emerged or even when our particular states were founded. But if I cannot, therefore, give my *explicit* consent to the provisions of the social contract, I nevertheless give them my *tacit* consent by remaining in my society and enjoying its benefits, rather than leaving. With the introduction of tacit consent, questions such as whether there ever actually existed a state of nature and whether people actually signed a social contract become irrelevant. Whatever the historical facts, what is crucial now is that we, ourselves, tacitly sign the social contract every day by remaining in civil society, thereby justifying the government's authority over us.

It might be objected that, if in Locke's time there were still enough uninhabited regions of the world that people could actually leave civil society, this is no longer true. Even if I renounce my national citizenship, I can still only go to some other country with an established government. Hence, I have no way of opting out of civil society altogether, which means my continued presence in civil society does not indicate my tacit consent to any government's authority. To this it must be replied that physically departing one's country is not the only way one can opt out of civil society. I can also simply declare myself no longer to be a member of my society and to be unbound by its laws. Withdrawing my consent from the government, I return to the state of nature. Of course, the state will not take my pronouncement lightly, especially if I begin actually breaking its laws. It will use its superior power to apprehend and punish me. I might complain, "The state has no right to punish me according to its laws, since I have not consented to them." But my complaint falls flat, for I am trying to invoke my rights against the state, when I have already renounced any civil relation to the state. Indeed, when I declare that I will actively defy the state, I effectively declare war on it. And since the state of war is governed only by the law of force, I have no grounds for complaint when the state uses its superior force to subdue me, in the interest of preserving itself. If I am willing to face the state's wrath, or believe I can avoid it, I may opt out of civil society. That I do not implies I tacitly give the government my consent.

Drawing out the full implications of the doctrine of tacit consent, Locke notes that, not just individuals, but the people *en masse* can always revoke their consent of the government. Indeed, Locke argues, people have a right and even a moral imperative to revolt against tyrannical governments. This right to revolution is not a civic right; no state can freely permit its people to engage in armed revolt, since the state is founded precisely to replace violence with stability. The right to revolt against tyranny is rather a natural right, stemming from the natural right of each individual citizen to resist enslavement. Before revolt becomes justified, Locke cautions, the government must commit a long pattern of serious abuses, and the people should exhaust all legal means of redress. But when a government systematically and chronically oppresses its people, it fails to uphold its end of the social contract, so the people have a right, not just to withdraw their active support of the government but to enter into a state of war with it and seek its overthrow. When revolution breaks out, neither side is bound by any rights or laws, since both are fighting for their survival. Who wins depends on who can muster the greatest force. The government will naturally have accumulated a great deal of power, especially if it has an army at its command. But the people will always outnumber the leaders, so if a rebel movement can gain strong public support, it stands a chance of success. In any case, should the rebels extra-legally oust the leaders or topple the whole political system, forging a new society requires concluding a new social contract, the old one having been torn up, first by the tyrannical government, then by the revolutionaries.

The Lockean Legacy

It is interesting that, despite the term "Glorious Revolution," when James II fled to France, Parliament was careful to specify that he had abdicated the throne, rather than having been driven from it. This meant William of Orange could simply move into an empty position within the established English government; no new social contract had to be concluded, since civil society had not been dissolved. Nevertheless, by inviting William to England, thereby encouraging James's "abdication," the English people and Parliament clearly signaled they had come to believe a people has the right to revolt against a king who abuses his public trust. The *Second Treatise of Government* established the theoretical basis of this view, thereby adding legitimacy to William's ascent to the throne. That Locke's political theory became the accepted account of political legitimacy in late seventeenth- and eighteenth-century England is hardly surprising, for Locke took the political values most politically-active Englishmen already agreed on and gave them a strong theoretical foundation: limited monarchy, respect for individual rights, the separation of powers, and the right to revolt against tyrants.

Most of the framers of the American Constitution were well-read men familiar with political philosophers ranging from Plato and Cicero to Hobbes and Montesquieu. Like their English counterparts, however, they viewed Locke as *the* standard authority on questions of political legitimacy, so when they use phrases like "consent of the governed" or "inalienable rights," it is Locke they are invoking. We now jump across the Atlantic to see how these former English subjects came to institutionalize Lockean contract theory and natural right doctrine—including the right to bear arms, which first came into being in England as Locke was writing the *Second Treatise*—in their constitution.

CHAPTER 4

The Right to Bear Arms: American Origins

In 1607, a group of English colonists landed in Jamestown and founded the first permanent European settlement in North America. Over the next century and a half, many other colonists followed, seeking religious freedom, economic opportunity, adventure, or an alternative to prison. Most came from the British Isles, but others came from northern Europe, and many slaves were imported from Africa. Eventually, thirteen English colonies were established along the central eastern edge of North America. Meanwhile, French settlers moved into the Canadian territories to the north, and Spain took control of most of the lands to the south, from Florida down through South America. Native American tribes were pushed ever further west, sometimes selling their lands, sometimes being driven from them. By 1776, the English colonies had declared their independence from the mother country, although six years of war were required to actually achieve independence. When the leaders of the newly-formed United States of America came to draft their own Constitution and Bill of Rights, they drew heavily on English history and political thought, though replacing the stuffy monarchy and aristocracy with a much more open system of democratic republicanism. The early colonists had also brought the English right to bear arms with them across the

Atlantic. This right, however, took on a new tenor in its new sur-
roundings.

Guns in the Colonies

The American colonists were a frontier people, exposed not only to
the dangers of nature but also to attack by the Native Americans they
were displacing. Guns were consequently a part of everyday life for
many colonists. Although the colonies were subject to English law,
the restrictions the English Bill of Rights had placed on gun ownership
were applied only loosely in the New World. The young colonies were
hardly models of religious tolerance, but so many settlers had come to
America seeking religious freedom that restricting gun ownership on
the basis of religion, though sometimes done, was difficult to justify.
The forests, moreover, were so vast and full of game that firearms did
not need to be regulated for the sake of preserving the hunt. Most of
the colonies did maintain a property requirement for gun ownership,
but it was minimal compared to that in England. Indeed, while some
colonists were wealthier than other, and some landowners—especially
in the South—liked to view themselves as forming a gentry, the English system of hereditary nobility never took root in America, so the
social structure did not arise by which gun ownership could be restricted on the basis of "condition." And as far as guns being permitted only "as allowed by law," all the colonies passed laws encouraging
or requiring gun ownership rather than restricting it. Connecticut law
stipulated, for instance, that every householder

> always be provided with and have in continual readiness, a well-fixed fire-
> lock...or other good fire-arms...a good sword, or cutlass...one pound of
> good powder, four pounds of bullets fit for his gun, and twelve flints.[1]

The one glaring restriction the colonies placed on gun ownership was
racial: black slaves were not permitted to bear arms, and selling firearms to a Native American was in some cases a capital offense. For
community defense, the colonies adopted the English institutions of
the hue and cry, watch and ward, and *posse comitatus*. Furthermore,
all the colonies formed militias, with every able-bodied male being
liable for service and required to report to musters properly armed.

These militias fell under the command of the British general responsible for North America, but the lower-ranking officers were local men.

Just because most white males were required to own guns, however, does not mean they actually did. In fact, an academic dispute has recently broken out concerning the prevalence of guns in colonial America, spurred by publication of Michael Bellesiles's *Arming America*. Bellesiles argues that there were far fewer guns in the colonies than popular belief, and most other historians, would maintain. Not surprisingly, other historians have sharply criticized this thesis, but it deserves a brief presentation here. Bellesiles explains that gun ownership was relatively rare in early America, except for among the upper classes, for two primary reasons. First, all guns were handcrafted at the time, and since virtually no gun production took place in the colonies prior to the Revolution, all guns had to be brought over from Europe. This made the cost of a gun prohibitive for most colonists—a musket cost the equivalent of two months' earnings for the average farmer or laborer.[2] It was not until Samuel Colt began mass-producing revolvers in the 1840's that guns became affordable to the average American. Secondly, most colonists simply did not have much need for a bulky, unreliable, rust-prone musket. Few colonists hunted. They had brought domesticated livestock from Europe, and raising chickens or pigs is a far more efficient means of putting meat on the table than hunting; those colonists who did hunt generally favored trapping. Moreover, given the inaccuracy, limited range, propensity to misfire, and lengthy loading time of seventeenth- and eighteenth-century muskets, the gun had not yet established itself as a terribly effective weapon for defending oneself or the community against Indians or anyone else. Many colonists therefore preferred to rely on swords or axes for their self-defense.

A second thesis Bellesiles advances, this one much less controversial, is that the colonial militias were hardly the rugged defense forces, composed of every man bearing his musket, that popular belief makes them out to be. In fact, throughout the colonial period, the militias were chronically short of guns; militia service was highly unpopular, and training was abysmal.[3] To illustrate the sorry state of the colonial militias, Bellesiles reports that in 1690, the colonies of New York, Massachusetts, and Connecticut had 10,000 men eligible for militia service between them. But when French and Indian forces from Canada made incursions into New England, burning forts and slaughtering men, only 255 colonists, plus 120 allied Indians, could be mustered to respond. Bellesiles describes the resulting campaign:

> It was a rather pathetic army, though still larger than any of the forces that had attacked from Canada. But the Colonial commanders forgot to arrange for boats to take their forces down Lake Champlain, so they turned back after burning La Prairie.[4]

The quality of the militia did improve slightly during the Seven Years War. In fighting between British and French forces in the upper Ohio Valley from 1754–63, colonial militia units served alongside British regulars, occasionally with distinction. In any case, American soldiers and officers gained a taste of the European style of combat that would characterize the Revolutionary War. Moreover, the British government made a concerted effort to better arm the colonial militias and thus shipped thousands of muskets across the Atlantic—muskets American soldiers would soon begin firing upon British troops.

The Rumblings of Revolution

Until 1763, relations between the American colonies and the mother country—which had become Great Britain in 1707 through the union of England, Wales, and Scotland—were smooth and mutually agreeable. As Britain's largest trading partner, the American colonies were the most valuable jewel in the British Empire. And while the colonies were governed by charters that kept them under the control of the British crown and Parliament, British rule was welcome, not resented, in America. Most importantly, British troops provided defense against the French to the north, the Indians to the west, and the Spaniards to the south. Most of the colonies had royally-appointed governors who could veto legislation, but each colony had an elected legislature that was given wide latitude to establish the laws of the colony. Furthermore, Great Britain had never taxed her American possessions. A series of Navigation Acts did stipulate that all colonial imports and exports had to be carried on British or American ships, and these ships had to pass through British ports, so the colonies could not trade directly with other nations. But if this raised the cost of doing business for some colonial merchants, most colonial trade would have been with Britain, anyway, and since the Navigation Acts protected this trade against foreign competition, few Americans complained about the Navigation Acts.

In 1763, the Treaty of Paris was signed to end the Seven Years War, which had engulfed much of Europe, and spilled over into the fighting between Britain and France in North America. Great Britain had won a decisive victory over both France and Spain. In accord with the Treaty of Paris, France renounced all claims to Canada and ceded most of Louisiana east of the Mississippi River to Britain, while Spain gave up Florida in exchange for the conquered Havana. The end of the Seven Years War brought about no immediate change in relations between Britain and her American colonies; certainly, no one could have predicted a war for colonial independence would break out in just over a decade. Nevertheless, the pullout of French and Spanish forces set the stage for rising tensions between the colonies and the mother country. The two principal military threats to the colonies were now gone. Only the Indians remained, and the colonial militias, familiar with the Indian style of fighting, were better equipped to deal with this threat than the European-trained redcoats. Yet, Britain was not inclined to withdraw her troops from America, as keeping the colonies dependent on military support had allowed Britain to win a certain amount of deference from her colonies. British policy makers did not foresee any immediate moves for American independence, but they knew a general military withdrawal could eventually lead in this direction. Hence, 8500 British soldiers were left in America, many of them posted at forts scattered along the frontier. Meanwhile, a small naval fleet was stationed at Halifax, Nova Scotia, ostensibly to defend the colonies against foreign enemies but also to help British customs officials enforce the Navigation Acts.

Indeed, though victorious in the Seven Years War, Britain was struggling to pay off her war debts, which resulted in extremely high domestic tax rates. And now that North America was no longer a theater of war, it did not seem fair to members of Parliament that the colonies should enjoy the protection of the British military without contributing anything to the maintenance of the empire, nay, without even helping to pay for their own protection. Thus, Parliament, anxious to lower taxes at home, resolved to transfer some of the cost of military protection to the colonies. In 1764, enforcement of the Navigation Acts was stepped up, and higher duties were collected on molasses, essential to making rum. In 1765, Parliament revised the

Mutiny Act to apply it to North America. This required the colonies to provide quarters for troops stationed in settled areas and to supply them with beer, firewood, candles, wagons, and other necessities. Many colonists immediately objected to the Mutiny Act, since it forced the colonial legislatures to apportion money for troops they had never requested and no longer wanted.

What really infuriated the colonists, however, was another act passed in the same session of Parliament, the Stamp Act. This act required the purchase of a government stamp for a wide number of goods and activities, from office paper to dice to setting sail for Europe. Revenues generated from the sale of stamps in the colonies would then be used to defray the cost of the British military presence. For the first time, colonists began raising strong vocal opposition to British policy. The fiery orator, Patrick Henry, pushed a series of anti-British resolutions through the Virginia House of Burgesses, and a number of other colonial legislatures followed suit. The chief complaint of the colonists was that both the Mutiny and Stamp Acts constituted taxation without representation. A fundamental provision of the English Constitution, dating back to the Magna Carta, holds that a person may only be taxed by a legislature in which that person participates or is represented. The Navigation Acts, intended to protect British shipping interests more than to generate revenues, could be defended as legitimate trade restrictions. The Mutiny and Stamp Acts, however, were both clearly designed for the sole purpose of transferring wealth from the colonies to Britain, and they were imposed by a British Parliament in which the colonies had no seats. The colonists therefore argued that their constitutional rights as British subjects were being trampled.

The first significant action the colonists took to resist British authority was to refuse to buy the required stamps. Outside of Georgia, a colony heavily subsidized by Britain, not a single stamp was ever sold. Meanwhile, colonists who accepted royal appointments as stamp distributors were socially ostracized, and in some cases physically abused. An embarrassing failure, the Stamp Act was rescinded in 1766. Parliament quickly came back, however, with a series of new taxes and other restrictive measures, determined not just to wring some tax monies from the colonies but to assert its prerogative to do so. In 1767, import duties were placed on products including tea, paint, lead, and paper. In 1768, an admiralty court was established in Halifax to try violators of the Navigation Acts, with verdicts being rendered by a single judge, rather than a jury of the defendant's peers. That same year, most of the British troops were moved from their frontier posts to various settled areas along the eastern seaboard. The irony of this move was not lost on the colonists. Troops on the East Coast could not very well protect the colonies against French, Spanish, or Indian attacks. The only purpose they could serve there would be to check any colonial moves towards independence. Meanwhile, the colonies were being forced to pay more for this "protection."

The colonists reacted with a widespread boycott of British products. To avoid acquiescing to the British tea duty, conscientious patriots made sure they drank tea smuggled in from Dutch sources. In Boston, moreover—the city that would become the focal point of colonial resistance—customs officials were physically harassed. British authorities responded by sending soldiers into the city. There was no immediate violence, and Parliament actually rescinded all of the import duties, with the exception of that on tea, in an attempt to diffuse the situation. But tensions continued to simmer in Boston, until March 1770, when a group of British soldiers, backed into a corner by an angry mob, panicked and opened fire, killing five and wounding seven in the infamous "Boston Massacre."

Tensions eased again somewhat when Britain quickly pulled her troops out of Boston, and the American boycott was scaled back to cover only tea. Increasingly, however, colonists began seeing themselves as being fundamentally wronged by Great Britain. When the Stamp Act was decried as unconstitutional, colonists were complaining that their rights as British subjects were being violated. Hence, they were still seeking redress within the British constitutional system. But when Richard Bland, in his *Enquiry into the Rights of the British Colonies*, argued that Britain's taxation of the colonists without their consent violated the colonists' natural right to hold private property, he was suggesting the British government was violating natural law, and hence the very social contract. And according to Lockean doctrine, when a government engages in a long pattern of such abuses, and all means legal of redress have been exhausted, revolution becomes, not just permissible but morally imperative.

In the early 1770's, few colonists were yet thinking seriously of revolting against Great Britain. But the actions of some colonists were becoming ever more revolutionary in character. In a successful effort to prevent the importation of British tea, colonists held a series of "tea parties" in American harbors, either turning away British merchant ships or boarding them and dumping their cargos of tea overboard. The first and most famous tea party took place in Boston in 1773, with around 340 chests of tea, worth £9000, being tossed into Boston harbor. The British responded by shutting down Boston harbor, moving 4000 troops into the city, disarming all Bostonians who wanted to leave the city, and reorganizing the Massachusetts legislature to allow British authorities to hand-pick its delegates. The popularly elected legislature met anyway and declared itself the colony's legal governing body, while taking command of the Massachusetts militia. As British troops sealed off Boston, militia units began gathering arms in the surrounding areas, and teams of "minutemen" were organized to respond quickly to emergencies. Meanwhile, all the colonies but Georgia heeded calls from both Massachusetts and Virginia to send delegates to a Continental Congress in Philadelphia. The First Continental Congress began meeting in September 1774 and pledged mutual support in the face of British aggression, as well as issuing a Declaration of Rights that based itself on both the English Constitution and the doctrine of natural right.

War Breaks Out

By 1775, officials in London had decided Britain needed to take strong action to put down the Massachusetts rebellion. In April, General Thomas Gage sent 700 soldiers marching toward Concord, Massachusetts to destroy military supplies the colonists had amassed there. On the way, in Lexington, the British troops encountered a band of 70 to 80 minutemen. Shots were fired, and eight minutemen were killed, compared to one redcoat wounded. The amateur American soldiers had simply been outnumbered and outclassed by the well-drilled British soldiers. By the time the redcoats began their return march to Boston, however, several thousand militia had lined the roads leading to the city. Firing at the British columns from behind trees and stone fences, the colonists inflicted heavy casualties on the redcoats. That the British troops made it back to Boston, at all, was only due to a relief party coming out to meet them with several artillery pieces as well as a complete lack of order on the American side. Gage held onto

Boston for a few more months, then removed his troops to Halifax until reinforcements could be brought across the Atlantic, and the War for Independence would begin in earnest.

Meeting in the summer of 1775, the Second Continental Congress ordered the formation of the Continental Army and placed George Washington in command. Growing out of the colonial militias, the Continental Army initially had the ragtag appearance of a militia: most soldiers wore civilian clothes, some carried their own muskets, and units were sorely lacking in training and discipline. General Washington, however, quickly moved to professionalize his forces and procure military supplies. As the war progressed, the Continental Army hardened into a professional fighting force that was probably comparable in quality to the British army. Militia units also continued to be used throughout the war, and if militiamen were more prone to flee in the face of British bayonet charges than army regulars, they materially augmented American numbers in several key battles. The colonial militias even played a significant role in the war effort when they were not in service. British troops had little difficulty establishing several strongholds along the eastern seaboard, but British planners realized the army would have to take control of large parts of the continent's interior if the American rebellion was to be crushed. British generals in the field, however, knew the farther inland they marched, the more colonists would take up arms, seeing their homes threatened. Any advancing British army would consequently risk getting trapped or having its supply lines cut by a militia springing up behind it. The British never attempted a major inland offensive.

Without going into a blow-by-blow account of the war, beginning in 1776, the Americans began receiving assistance from France, eager to strike a blow back at England. After several years of stalemate, French money and military supplies, and later soldiers and ships, tipped the balance in favor of the Americans. In October 1781, the headstrong young British general, Lord Cornwallis, got pinned down at Yorktown, Pennsylvania, by French and American troops, with the French navy blocking escape by sea. The British troops were forced to lay down their arms before General Washington. Fighting continued elsewhere, but the back of the British fighting force had been broken. A year later, Benjamin Franklin, John Adams, and John Jay signed a peace treaty in Paris by which Great Britain recognized the full independence and sovereignty of the United States of America.

Crafting a New Society

The American Revolution was fought by colonists seeking independence from imperial rule. But the leaders of the Revolution knew they were also fighting a war of ideals, and if they achieved independence from Britain yet allowed tyranny to arise in America, the sacrifices of the Revolution would have been wasted. In July of 1776, with British troops still massing at Halifax, the Continental Congress issued the Declaration of Independence. In the second sentence of the Declaration, author Thomas Jefferson gives a remarkable summary of natural right doctrine and contract theory.

> We hold these truths to be self-evident, that all Men are created equal, that they are endowed by their Creator with certain unalienable Rights, that among these are Life, Liberty, and the Pursuit of Happiness—That to secure these Rights, Governments are instituted among Men, deriving their Just Powers from the Consent of the Governed...

Continuing this sentence, Jefferson invokes the Lockean right to revolution.

> that whenever any Form of Government becomes destructive of these Ends, it is the right of the People to alter or abolish it, and to institute a new Government.

Jefferson follows Locke in stressing that a prudent people will suffer many minor injuries before moving against its government. He maintains, however, that the colonies had suffered such "a long Train of Abuses and Usurpations" that revolt against Britain had become both justified and necessary.

> Such has been the patient Sufferance of these Colonies; and such is now the Necessity which constrains them to alter their former Systems of Government. The History of the present King of Great Britain is a History of repeated Injuries and Usurpations, all having in direct Object the Establishment of an absolute Tyranny over these States.

To support this charge of tyranny, Jefferson lists 28 abuses the colonies had suffered at the hands of Great Britain, laying the blame directly on George III. Included on the list of grievances are several referring to the British military presence:

He [George] has kept among us, in Times of Peace, Standing Armies, without the consent of our Legislatures.

He has effected to render the Military independent of and superior to the Civil Power.

[He has assented to legislation] For quartering large Bodies of Armed Troops among us.

These grievances make clear that, if the colonists may have viewed taxation without representation as the most objectionable manifestation of British tyranny, they had inherited the English belief that a standing army is the tyrant's most effective instrument of oppression.

The colonies were governed by royal charters, so when they declared independence, their charters became meaningless. Hence, even as British troops poured back onto American soil, all thirteen of the states now comprising the United States of America drafted and ratified state constitutions. These constitutions differed in their details, but all established representative governments that divided power among separate legislative, executive, and judicial bodies. None of the states established a monarchy, and none institutionalized anything resembling the British system of hereditary nobility, though all the states maintained property requirements for voting. Many states attached bills of rights to their constitutions, the constitution proper mapping out the structure of the state government, and the bill of rights enumerating the individual or collective rights the state would protect. Several such bills contained articles stressing the preferability of citizen militias to standing armies. The Virginia Bill of Rights, for example, maintains,

That a well regulated militia, composed of the body of the people, trained to arms, is the proper, natural, and safe defense of a free state: that standing armies in time of peace, should be avoided, as dangerous to liberty; and that in all cases the military should be under strict subordination to, and governed by, the civil power.

A few states explicitly recognized the right of citizens to bear arms. Framers in North Carolina and Massachusetts, for instance, both proclaimed, "That the people have a right to bear arms for the defense of the state," while the Pennsylvania Declaration of Rights asserts,

"That the people have a right to bear arms for the defense of themselves and the state." New Jersey, New York, South Carolina, and Georgia all declined to enact bills of rights, on the argument that such documents are unnecessary and perhaps even dangerous: a bill of rights can only enumerate natural rights, which people enjoy even before they enter civil society. For the state to list these inalienable rights in an official document wrongly suggests that the state can regulate them.

Following independence, not only did the states need to form governments for themselves, so did the new union. As the war progressed, the question remained open as to how closely the states would unite—whether they would essentially form a confederation of sovereign states, or come together as a single nation-state. General sentiment seemed to favor loose confederacy, but the war was forcing at least a degree of unity on the states. In 1777, the Continental Congress enacted the Articles of Confederation, which formally joined the states together in a "firm league of friendship." The new Confederation Congress was given some legislative powers over the states, although not over individual citizens. Thus, the Congress could request money from the states, but it could not tax individuals; only the state governments could do this. Intent on preventing either the national or state governments from slipping into tyranny, the drafters of the Articles adopted the traditional English policy of prioritizing the militia over the professional army. Hence, even as the Continental Army was desperately trying to expel what had become a foreign invader, the Articles forbade states to maintain standing armies during peacetime, "except such number only, as in the judgment of the United States in Congress assembled, shall be deemed requisite to garrison the forts necessary for the defense of such state." At the same time, the Articles proclaimed that every state "shall always keep up a well-regulated and disciplined militia, sufficiently armed and accoutered." No mention was made of an individual right to bear arms, the regulation of individual conduct being left to the states.

Written in time of war, the Articles of Confederation were undeniably flawed. Most critically, though Article XIII decrees "the Articles of this Confederation shall be inviolably observed by every State," the Articles contained no enforcement mechanisms—they were a Hobbesian covenant without the sword. Thus, while the Confederation Congress could request money from the states, it was helpless if they declined to contribute. As a result, the national government was constantly short of funds. Moreover, lawmaking was difficult, since passing most bills required the vote of nine out of thirteen states, and amendments to the Articles themselves needed the consent of all thirteen states. Despite the weakness of the Articles, the confederation held together of necessity throughout the war. Once the Revolution was over, however, many observers quickly realized the weak national government established by the Articles would be incapable of managing the many problems facing the young nation, including debt, inflation, Spanish and Indian threats, and chaotic interstate relations. Former royalists at home and cynics in Europe publicly doubted the United States would be able to maintain its republican principles for long, arguing that only a strong monarch could hold together such a large country.

The Constitution

In 1786, a convention was called in Annapolis to discuss ways of encouraging the free flow of interstate commerce. But only twelve delegates, representing five states, showed up—not enough to conduct the scheduled business. Still, the meeting produced important results. Largely at the instigation of James Madison, Alexander Hamilton authored a letter calling for another convention, this one to be held the following spring in Philadelphia, for the purpose of discussing all matters necessary "to render the constitution of the federal government adequate to the exigencies of the Union." The Confederation Congress grudgingly approved the proposed convention, though authorizing it only to consider ways of revising the Articles of Confederation.

Madison paid little heed to the congressional stipulation. Knowing the Articles to be fundamentally flawed, he had spent the previous year poring over the works of the most important classical and modern political theorists, while developing his own ideas on government. When delegates from enough states had trickled into Philadelphia to make a quorum, Madison's Virginia delegation presented them with a fully developed plan for a new constitution. Taken aback, most of the delegates doubted they had the authority to even discuss a new constitution. The Virginians gradually convinced them, however, that saving the union would require more than tinkering with the Articles of Confederation, and that if they did not seize the present moment, they might not get another chance to peacefully revise their form of government. Madison's "Virginia Plan" was by no means accepted as proposed, but it served as the basis for discussions that would drag out over five months, as the delegates hammered out a new constitution. In September 1787, the Constitutional Convention agreed on a final draft, and the proposed constitution was sent out to the states for ratification.

Serious divisions often brought the Convention to a standstill, but the delegates were guided by a common motive in their deliberations: they wanted to craft a system of government that was stronger than the present national government, yet would structurally prevent the emergence of tyranny. Hamilton, a proponent of constitutional monarchy, made one early speech advocating the appointment of a president-for-life, but his proposal received no support. More serious arguments were put forth for some sort of oligarchy, where high property requirements for voting and office holding would ensure that the country be governed by large landowners, presumably the best educated and soberest members of society. Certainly, none of the delegates advocated a pure democracy, which would allow the people to vote on every matter of importance to them. Not only would this be impracticable in such a large nation, but the delegates knew the masses to be too fickle and prone to faction to be entrusted with direct governance. Still, the delegates remembered that in Britain, not just the king, but also the gentry exercised a tyranny over the common people through its combined political and economic power. Property requirements therefore gradually fell out of the debate. In the end, a consensus emerged for a system of representative democracy, with eligibility for both voting and office holding being extended to as many citizens as practical, that is, to most white males.

From Locke, the framers had learned the best strategy for crafting a government that allows for effective governance yet is resistant to tyranny is to separate power among distinct individuals and institutions. From the French philosopher Montesquieu, they got the further idea of granting each branch of government specific powers allowing it to check the powers of the other branches, thereby ensuring that institutional jealously would preserve a balance of power among the various branches. Accordingly, the Constitution divides legislative, executive, and judicial powers among three distinct branches of government, with a carefully crafted system of checks and balances preventing any one branch from dominating the others. For instance, only Congress can pass a law. The President then has the power to veto the law, although Congress can override a presidential veto with a two-thirds majority. The courts are then called on to apply the laws to specific cases, and occasionally they overturn laws as failing to comply with the Constitution.[5] Beyond separating powers within the federal government, the Constitution divides power between the federal and state governments. Finally, at the deepest level, power is split between the government and the people: the government is invested with the power it needs to govern, but the people retain the ultimate check of being able to vote their leaders out of office.

Not surprisingly, the issue of standing armies came up for debate at the Constitutional Convention. Elbridge Gerry wanted to include a provision in the Constitution prohibiting the federal government from maintaining a standing army during peacetime. The Americans had learned first hand how much a standing army can bolster the power of a tyrannical government. Moreover, Europe lay across the ocean, so the United States was hardly liable to surprise attack; there would be plenty of time to assemble an army if war appeared immanent. Finally, each state had its militia, and the militias had provided valuable service during the war. Thus, the state militias could anchor the national defense, and there would be no need for a federal army during peacetime.

Madison reports that when Gerry had finished his speech, General Washington leaned over and facetiously whispered to a colleague that he was going to propose another amendment, that no foreign army be allowed to invade the United States with over 3000 troops.[6] The other delegates shared Washington's sentiments. Even if the colonial militias had played an important role in the war—a notion some disputed, especially Washington—the militias could not have won the war alone. The professional Continental Army, aided by French regulars, had been needed to defeat the experienced British troops. And while the Continental Army had only been assembled at the outbreak of war, it had also fared poorly its first few years. A professional army maintained during peacetime would be better prepared to fight the inevitable next war than an army thrown together at the last minute. Nor was the United States really isolated geographically: Great Britain had retained control of Canada, Spain still held the mouth of the Mississippi River, and the Indian threat remained to the west.

Hence, though all the delegates were leery of standing armies, they unanimously voted not to tie the hands of future governments facing unforeseeable dangers by prohibiting them from maintaining a standing army during peacetime. The delegates did, however, seek to blunt the military as a possible instrument of oppression by placing it firmly in civilian hands and spreading out its control. The President was made Commander-in-Chief of the military, but Congress was given control of its funding, as well as the sole power to declare war. With respect to the militia, Article I, Section 8 of the Constitution empowers the federal government,

> To provide for calling forth the militia to execute the laws of the union, suppress insurrections and repel invasions;

and,

> To provide for organizing, arming, and disciplining, the militia, and for governing such part of them as may be employed in the service of the United States, reserving to the states respectively, the appointment of the officers, and the authority of training the militia according to the discipline prescribed by Congress.

Thus, in the English tradition, the militia would be commanded by the central government, but its officers would be local citizens, in this case men appointed by the state governments.

The Bill of Rights

When the Constitution went out to the states for ratification, the complaint most frequently lodged against it was that it contained no bill of rights. Some "federalists," or supporters of the proposed Constitution, replied that the states would be capable of protecting the rights of their citizens, most states already having their own bills of rights. Other federalists, echoing the arguments of several states, warned that a federal bill of rights would be dangerous, in that it would wrongly suggest the federal government could regulate inalienable natural rights. And what would be the status of those natural rights that missed enumeration? Madison agreed that a bill of rights was not strictly necessary, natural rights remaining in effect even when not constitutionally protected. But he thought an enumeration of rights could do no harm, and it might even do some good by precisely fixing the limits of the federal government's power over the people. Moreover, enacting such a bill would be a conciliatory gesture that would win over most of the Constitution's "anti-federalist" opponents, so Madison and others pledged to push for a bill of rights in the next session of Congress if the Constitution was ratified. By the time the first Congress met under the Constitution in the spring of 1789, conventions in eleven states had ratified it. North Carolina ratified later that year, and Rhode Island finally entered the union in 1790. Many states ratified, however, only on the condition that certain proposed amendments be considered as soon as possible.

When Congress came into session, Representative Madison was given the task of compiling all the amendments the states had proposed and compressing them into a form more easily debated. He drew up nine amendments—Congress would ultimately send thirteen to the states—concerning such topics as freedom of speech, due process, search and seizure, and cruel and unusual punishment. Among these was the initial draft of what is now the Second Amendment. It read,

> The right of the people to keep and bear arms shall not be infringed; a well armed and well regulated militia being the best security of a free country; but no person religiously scrupulous of bearing arms shall be compelled to render military service in person.[7]

This amendment, along with the others, was referred to the House Committee on Amendments, which made a few stylistic changes. When brought to the floor of the House, the amendment concerning the right to bear arms received little debate, compared to other amendments. Most of the discussion centered on the final clause, concerning exemption from military service for those with religious scruples. Gerry raised the following concern:

> I am apprehensive, sir, that this clause would give an opportunity to the people in power to destroy the constitution itself. They can declare who are those religiously scrupulous, and prevent them from bearing arms.[8]

Thus, while Madison doubtless included the "conscientious objector" clause out of respect for such non-violent sects as the Quakers, Gerry feared that mixing religion and gun privileges could lead to a repeat of

English history, where the right to bear arms had been used to discriminate against specific religions. Other representatives thought the
clause would be abused by people simply wishing to avoid military
service, whatever their religion. The clause was dropped. The House
passed the resulting amendment by the necessary two-thirds majority,
and sent it on to the Senate. The Senate did not yet record its debates,
so we know little of what was said in that chamber. A proposal was
made to add the words "for their common defense" immediately after
"the right to keep and bear arms," but the proposal was defeated.

By the time the amendment guaranteeing the right to bear arms
had won the approval of both houses, it had been modified to read,

> A well regulated Militia, being necessary to the security of a free State, the
> right of the people to keep and bear Arms, shall not be infringed.

The removal of the conscientious objector was substantive; all the
other changes, if significant, were clearly stylistic in nature. "A well
regulated militia" was moved to the beginning of the sentence, likely
for emphasis. "Well armed" was dropped as a qualifier of "militia,"
presumably because an "armed militia" is redundant. The militia was
declared to be "necessary" to the security of a free state, rather than
merely being the state's "best security," so that "best security" would
not be construed as implying that replacing the militia with a standing
army was an acceptable defense strategy, if not the best possible. Finally, "free country" was changed to "free State." One unfortunate
result of all this cutting and pasting was that the resulting amendment
is a grammatical nightmare. The placement of the commas is mysti-
fying, and it is unclear whether the subject of the sentence is "Militia"
or "right." This latter unclarity, especially, has given rise to widely
divergent interpretations of the Second Amendment, since it leaves
the grammatical and legal function of the "militia clause" ambiguous:
Does this clause limit the right to bear arms to the context of militia
service, or does it merely state the most important justification for
protecting the right to bear arms? The language must have been clear
enough to members of the state legislatures, however, for by 1791,
the required three-fourths of the states had ratified the Second
Amendment, along with the rest of the Bill of Rights.

The right to keep and bear arms had become part of the fundamental law of the United States.

CHAPTER 5

Interpreting the Second Amendment

The Second Amendment was uncontroversial when drafted and remained uncontroversial until the twentieth century. The Supreme Court did not even issue a ruling directly invoking the Second Amendment until 1876. In the twentieth century, however, the Second Amendment became one of the most fiercely debated provisions in the entire Constitution. What is at stake in this debate, and how can we go about navigating it?

The Emergence of the Debate

The early lack of controversy surrounding the Second Amendment was mainly due to the fact that federal, state, and municipal governments placed very few restrictions on gun ownership until the twentieth century, the exception being various laws that restricted gun possession by ex-slaves after the Civil War. During the Prohibition years of 1919–33, gun crime exploded as gangsters trafficking in illegal alcohol used pistols, sawed-off shotguns, and machine guns to terrorize local businesses, police, and one another. This violence prompted passage of the National Firearms Act of 1934, which heavily taxed the manufacture and distribution of guns, while banning such especially dangerous firearms as sawed-off shotguns and machine guns. The Federal Firearms Act of 1938 then placed limits on the interstate shipment of guns, and prohibited shipping guns to felons. This act was later replaced by the Gun Control Act of 1968, which required the licensing of gun dealers, placed restrictions on interstate gun sales and gun importation, established penalties for the use of a firearm in the commission of a federal felony, and forbade private ownership of such "destructive devices" as bombs and grenades. The Firearms Owners' Protection Act of 1986 eased some of these restrictions on gun ownership, sales, and interstate shipping. In 1994, the Brady Bill established a five-day waiting period for the purchase of handguns, to give police time to complete background checks on purchasers. This same year saw passage of the Assault Weapons Ban, which prohibits the sale and manufacture of certain types of military-style semiautomatic weapons. Meanwhile, various states and municipalities have passed gun laws that do everything from banning handguns to requiring that all households be armed.

All of these restrictions on gun possession have prompted challenges to their constitutionality under the Second Amendment. As courts, legislative bodies, and the general public have debated the constitutionality of gun control, much of the debate has revolved around the question of whether the Second Amendment guarantees a collective right or an individual right, that is, whether it guarantees states the right to form militias, or individuals the right to own guns. Yet, the possible individual right to bear arms may itself be interpreted in two different ways, so three distinct interpretations of the Second Amendment have been widely advocated.

1. The Second Amendment guarantees states, as collectivities of citizens, the right to maintain well-regulated militias.

2. The Second Amendment guarantees individuals the right to keep and bear arms, but only in the context of possible militia service.

3. The Second Amendment guarantees individuals the right to keep and bear arms, without further restriction.

Thus, the first two possible interpretations consider the right to bear arms to be restricted to the context of militia service. The first, however, understands "the people" whose right is guaranteed to be the people of a state as a collectivity, whereas the second regards "the people" as individual people. The third possible interpretation denies there to be any such restriction, and thus maintains the Second Amendment protects private gun ownership for such purposes as collecting, target shooting, hunting, and especially self-defense, as well as militia service.

Which interpretation is correct? Practically speaking, answering this question requires looking to the records of the federal courts. According to the system of common law the United States inherited from England, when a court issues a ruling that articulates a particular interpretation of some law, a precedent is set, and the law is then understood to bear that legal meaning for all areas under the court's jurisdiction. This precedent can later be altered by the same court or a higher one, or the law can be amended or repealed by the legislature. Until one of these things happens, however, the law effectively means what the court decision says it means. We therefore turn to consider how federal courts have interpreted the Second Amendment.

The View of the Courts

Since 1876, federal courts have consistently ruled that the Second Amendment guarantees a collective right of states to form militias. The Supreme Court has not closed the door, however, to the possibility that the Second Amendment also guarantees an individual right. The seminal decision is *United States v. Miller* (1934), and it is ambiguous. In this case—which later decisions have reaffirmed[1]—the Supreme Court upheld the ban on sawed-off shotguns imposed by the National Firearms Act, noting that,

> in the absence of any evidence tending to show that possession or use of a "shotgun having a barrel of less than eighteen inches in length" at this time has some reasonable relationship to the preservation or efficiency of a well-regulated militia, we cannot say that the Second Amendment guarantees the right to keep and bear such an instrument. Certainly it is not within judicial notice that this weapon is any part of the ordinary military equipment or that its use could contribute to the common defense.

Proponents of both gun control and gun rights have claimed support from this ruling. Control advocates argue that the ruling establishes the Second Amendment to be exclusively concerned with the state militias. The Third Circuit Court of Appeals took this view in *United States v. Tot* (1942).

> [The Second Amendment,] unlike those providing for protection of free speech and freedom of religion, was not adopted with individual rights in mind, but as a protection for the States in the maintenance of their militia organizations against possible encroachment by the federal power.

Gun rights advocates note, however, that *Miller* seems to imply private arms ownership is protected, as long as the arms in question have a conceivable military use. And since virtually any firearm, from handgun to machine gun, could be of some conceivable use in a guerilla-style war fought against a tyrannical federal government, the Second Amendment must protect the private ownership of virtually all guns. No federal ruling has yet endorsed this interpretation, but neither has it been explicitly rejected.

Another key point to note here is that the Bill of Rights, as drafted, provided constitutional protection for the enumerated rights only against the federal government, not against state governments. That is, the First Amendment, for example, protected individuals against federal restrictions on free speech. The state governments, however, remained free to impose any limits on speech they wanted. The Fourteenth Amendment was ratified in 1868, primarily to ensure that the states treat all their citizens equally, but it also prohibits states from making laws that "shall abridge the privileges or immunities of citizens of the United States." In the twentieth century, federal courts gradually began to "incorporate" various rights from the Bill of Rights into the Fourteenth Amendment, thus protecting these rights against infringement by the state governments. In 1931, for instance, *Near v. Minnesota* incorporated the First Amendment freedom of the press into the Fourteenth Amendment, thereby prohibiting states from infringing the freedom of press of individuals or groups. To this point, *no federal ruling has incorporated the Second Amendment into the Fourteenth.* This indicates the federal courts do not presently interpret the Second Amendment as protecting individuals against state gun restrictions, whatever protection it may or may not provide individuals against federal restrictions. Indeed, if the Second Amendment merely guarantees the collective right of states to form militias, incorporation would make no sense, since incorporation protects individuals against states. Some gun advocates maintain the Fourteenth Amendment incorporates the entire Bill of Rights, thus implying that the Second Amendment must protect individuals against state gun restrictions. This claim, however, finds no support in federal case history, and it is directly contradicted by the practice of "selective incorporation" by which the Supreme Court has incorporated other rights one by one over the course of many decades.

Of course, with respect to the contemporary gun debate, the most pressing question is whether the federal courts have viewed gun control measures as constitutional under the Second Amendment. The Supreme Court has never explicitly stated that the principle of gun control is constitutionally sound. On the other hand, over the past century federal courts have not overturned a single federal, state, or local gun restriction on Second Amendment grounds, despite numerous challenges. In perhaps the most significant recent ruling, the Supreme Court in 1985 refused to hear an appeal seeking to overturn a handgun ban enacted by the township of Morton Grove, Illinois, thereby upholding the ban. Still, the Court does not give its reasons for refusing to hear cases, so in this case it is not clear whether the justices rejected the argument that the Second Amendment protects private gun ownership, or whether they held it does not provide protection against state or local restrictions.

In sum, then, the federal courts have leaned toward the view that the Second Amendment is exclusively a militia provision, and they have shown no willingness to limit the ability of federal, state, or local legislatures to enact gun control measures. Nevertheless, the Supreme Court has yet to offer a ruling that definitively establishes the meaning and scope of the Second Amendment. And since the Court could always overturn those rulings it has issued, the debate over the Second Amendment's interpretation continues, and it continues to be relevant.

Interpretive Strategy

Acknowledging that the debate over the Second Amendment's interpretation is still in progress, I will here consider the three possible interpretations listed above, to determine which are tenable interpretations of the Second Amendment. By "tenable," I mean an interpretation that may reasonably have been shared by most of those who drafted and ratified the amendment, whether or not federal courts have since adopted this interpretation. In part, therefore, determining tenability will require seeking out the intent of the framers by examining the text itself, the relevant historical documents, and the historical and intellectual backdrop against which the amendment was drafted. The previous chapter should have made clear, however, that there never was a single, univocal "intent of the framers." Between the actual drafting of the amendment and votes taken in the House, Senate, and state legislatures, literally hundreds of people took part in the ratification process, playing different institutional roles, representing different interests and ideas, and willing to compromise on different issues. Hence, the framers and ratifiers likely had many different intents with respect to the Second Amendment. In weighing the tenability of a particular interpretation, therefore, I will not just seek to determine the framers' intent as a historical matter. I will also pose the more theoretical question of whether the Second Amendment, so interpreted, would have made good constitutional sense at the time it was enacted, given the framers' historical context, the theory of government they were invoking, and their general, agreed-upon aims in drafting the Constitution and Bill of Rights. In other words, I will ask whether legislators in 1789 *should* have ratified the Second Amendment, assuming they understood it in terms of the interpretation in question.

I do not stop here, however. For those interpretations that pass the test of tenability, I will submit them to a second test: I will ask whether, on the interpretation in question, the Second Amendment still makes good sense today as a constitutional provision. Presumably we share the framers' theory of government and their general constitutional aims. But the historical context in which we live has undeniably changed, thus raising the possibility that an amendment which made good constitutional sense over two hundred years ago is now obsolete. If, at the end of the day, a tenable interpretation of the Second Amendment can be found that still makes good constitutional sense today, then we must advocate that the amendment be allowed to stand. But if we can find no interpretation that made good constitutional sense in 1789 and still makes good sense today, we must begin arguing for the Second Amendment's repeal, in the interest of keeping the Constitution strong by keeping it lean.

In the following chapter, I will consider the first two possible interpretations listed above, that is, those which limit the scope of the Second Amendment to the context of the state militias. Then, in Chapter 7, I will consider the third possible interpretation, which asserts an unrestricted individual right to bear arms.

CHAPTER 6

The Right to Bear Arms for Militia Service

Whatever else the framers of the Second Amendment may have intended, all evidence suggests their primary concern in drafting the amendment was to ensure that the states be able to form militias as a means of warding off tyranny by the federal government. But does this mean the right to keep and bear arms is a right of states to maintain arsenals for their militias? Or is it a right of individual citizens to own guns, so that they can report for militia service properly armed? In the contemporary gun debate, proponents of gun control typically argue that the Second Amendment ensures a collective right, whereas gun advocates maintain an individual right is guaranteed. In this chapter, I will defend the view that interpreting the Second Amendment as guaranteeing an individual right to bear arms for militia service is the most tenable interpretation of this amendment. I will go on to argue, however, that the Second Amendment has become just as obsolete as citizen militias, and hence it should be repealed, at least if its sole concern is guns owned for purposes of militia service. Again, discussion of the possible right to bear arms for other purposes will be put off until the next chapter.

Individual or Collective Right?

That the framers of the Second Amendment were intent on ensuring the ability of the states to form militias is undisputed. The strongest evidence for this intent is the text of the amendment, itself, which opens with the clause, "A well regulated Militia, being necessary to the security of a free State." Again, Madison had placed this clause at the end of his initial draft of the amendment. The House Committee on Amendments moved it to the beginning, thus emphasizing it, as well giving it more the appearance of a justificatory clause: the revised amendment appears to proclaim the right to bear arms shall not be infringed *because* a militia is necessary to the security of a free state. Any survey of the relevant historical literature further demonstrates that ensuring the ability of states to form militias was not just one purpose the framers had in drafting the Second Amendment, but their primary purpose. For mention of the right to bear arms is almost always accompanied by statements stressing the importance of an armed populace for blunting a government's ability to oppress its people by means of a standing army. To cite just a few examples, in a pamphlet advocating ratification of the Bill of Rights, Noah Webster writes,

> Before a standing army can rule, the people must be disarmed; as they are in almost every kingdom in Europe. The supreme power in America cannot enforce unjust laws by the sword, because the whole body of the people are armed, and constitute a force superior to any band of regular troops that can be, on any pretence, raised in the United States.[1]

And in a widely published editorial supporting the Bill of Rights, Tench Coxe writes,

> As civil rulers, not having their duty to the people before them, may attempt to tyrannize, and as the military forces which must be occasionally raised to defend our country, might pervert their power to the injury of their fellow-citizens, the people are confirmed by the next article [the Second Amendment] in their right to keep and bear their private arms.[2]

Indeed, for the framers to include in the Bill of Rights a provision promoting the state militias made excellent constitutional sense. The resounding message of the Constitution is, "We will not abide tyranny," and the Anglo-American tradition had long recognized citizen militias to be one of the most effective means of checking the power of a potentially tyrannical government. We could say the Second Amendment adds another check to the Constitution's system of checks and balances, this one a check of both the states and the people against the federal government, counterbalancing the federal military with the state militias.

If the primary concern of the framers was to ensure that the states be able to form militias, does this mean the Second Amendment guarantees states a collective right to form militias? Not necessarily. In fact, without even considering the amendment's text, it would have been surprising if the framers had wanted to enact an amendment granting states a constitutional right to form militias. After all, provision for the militia had already been made in the body of the Constitution, with the militia being placed under dual federal-state control. If the Second Amendment were merely to guarantee that states could form militias under this arrangement, what would the states have gained through the Second Amendment, over and above the partial control of the militias they already enjoy under the Constitution? And if the Second Amendment were to give states the right to form militias falling exclusively under their control, the dangerous possibility would arise of a state having two militias, one under federal-state control, the other under state control. Certainly, none of the framers could have had such a conflict-prone, as well as inefficient, arrangement in mind. If they had wanted to put militias exclusively under state control, they would have amended Article I, Section 8 of the Constitution, rather than using the Bill of Rights to create a second system of state militias.

The text of the Second Amendment lends strong support to the view that its framers intended to guarantee an individual, not a collective, right. Following the militia clause, the amendment explicitly proclaims, "the right of the people to keep and bear arms, shall not be infringed." Of course, the crucial question here is whether "the people" refers to a collectivity or individual people, and since this question lies at the heart of most Second Amendment debates, simply quoting the text provides no definitive answer one way or the other. Nevertheless, the amendment does use the term "state" in the militia clause, and "the people" in the guarantee clause, thus suggesting some distinction between the two; the Tenth Amendment similarly distinguishes between states and the people. Moreover, if the framers had wanted to ensure a collective right, it seems they could just as well have stipulated, "the right of states to raise and maintain militias shall not be infringed." That they instead guaranteed "the right of the people to keep and bear arms" strongly suggests they wanted to protect individuals. Incidentally, in the editorial cited above, Tench Coxe notes that the Second Amendment confirms the right of the people "to keep and bear their *private* arms [emphasis added]." Madison read Coxe's editorial approvingly, and thanked Coxe for his support.[3]

Further evidence that Madison and the other framers intended for "the people" to refer to individuals comes from the language used to invoke the right to bear arms. The Second Amendment does not proclaim that people "shall have the right" to keep and bear arms, but rather that this right "shall not be infringed." In other words, the amendment *guarantees* the right to bear arms, rather than *conferring* it. This indicates the framers believed the right to bear arms to be a natural right, such that the Constitution could only commit the government to upholding it; the Constitution could not confer a right upon people that they already possess in the state of nature and can never give up. Indeed, we have seen that one contemporary school of thought held natural rights to be the only type of right a bill of rights can protect. Madison would later point out that the ten amendments constituting the Bill of Rights actually protect a mixed bag of rights, some natural and some constitutionally conferred. The right to trial by jury, for instance, is a fundamental civic right under English common law, but it cannot be a natural right, since there are no courts or juries in the state of nature. Still, the language used in the Second Amendment indicates that the framers believed the right to bear arms to be one of those rights that people naturally and inalienably possess.

On this point, the framers were probably following William Blackstone, whose *Commentaries on the Laws of England* had become the standard legal reference in the English-speaking world by the time of the Revolution. Blackstone maintains that the right to bear arms is a natural right, derived from the natural right to self-defense: having the right to defend our lives, we must have the right to equip ourselves for this purpose.[4] For Blackstone, both the right to self-defense and the derivative right to bear arms are expressly individual rights. Consequently, when the framers of the Second Amendment used language to guarantee, rather than confer, the right to bear arms, it is likely they had an individual, natural right in mind.

Might the framers have intended to guarantee an individual right to bear arms but also a collective right of states to form militias? This is possible, although when we take into account the Second Amendment's language of guarantee, it becomes very difficult to wring a collective right out of the Second Amendment. Any collective right of states to form militias would have to be a civic right, not a natural right, for the militia, like trial by jury, is a civic institution that does not exist in the state of nature. Moreover, even if a group of people were somehow to form a militia in the state of nature, their freedom to do so is not a natural right, for people may perfectly well give up this freedom when they enter civil society, as evidenced by the fact that most nations have nothing resembling the institution of the militia; far more common is universal conscription in the regular military. Consequently, if the Second Amendment does invoke a collective right of states to form militias, it can only confer this right, not guarantee it. One may choose to argue the Second Amendment does, in fact, confer such a collective right, but this undeniably grates against the amendment's language. Interpreting the amendment as guaranteeing an individual right to bear arms accords much better with both the amendment's language and the natural right doctrine it invokes.

Yet, if the primary concern of the framers was to ensure the ability of states to form militias, why did they guarantee an individual right to bear arms, rather than expressly conferring a collective right upon the states? Given the history of the institution of the militia, the framers likely viewed private gun ownership as essential to any militia. Hence, by guaranteeing individuals the right to bear arms, the framers were seeking to ensure the presence of *conditions* under which states could always form militias.

In both England and the colonies, reporting for musters properly armed had always been a key component of one's militia duty. In England, the fact that citizens supplied their own weapons had been one of the main reasons the crown accepted the militia as the anchor of England's national defense—this arrangement was much cheaper than equipping a standing army. Yet, the arrangement also allowed the militia to fulfill its secondary role of maintaining a check on royal power. When the king called out the militia for some unpopular cause, the people could always frustrate his plans by showing up for musters either unarmed or with shoddy weapons. And if the king acted tyrannically enough, the people could take up arms against him, using their own guns. The English had already done so twice, although in the second instance the mere threat of a rebellious, armed populace had been enough to drive James from the throne. Privately armed militia units likewise played a role in America's overthrow of tyranny. Notably, privately owned guns helped discourage British troops from ever mounting a major inland campaign, since whenever the British did advance, well-armed militia units seemed to well up out of the ground behind them, threatening their supply lines. That Americans continued to believe private arms to be essential to the institution of the militia, even after the Revolution, is evidenced by the fact that the Militia Act of 1792 stipulates that the militia should consist of all able-bodied males, supplying their own arms. Indeed, the act gave men six months to obtain the required muskets.

Granting that militias traditionally depended on private arms ownership, why did the framers feel they had to go to the lengths of constitutionally protecting individuals against federal gun restrictions? They must have envisioned something like the following scenario. The federal government, having designs on tyranny, bans private gun ownership nationwide. Then, as allowed by Article I, Section 8 of the Constitution, which makes the federal government responsible for equipping the militia, the government pulls all militia weapons out of the state armories. Patrick Henry worried about just such a possibility at the Virginia constitutional convention when he asked,

> Of what service would militia be to you when, most probably, you will not have a single musket in the state? For, as arms are to be provided by Congress, they may or may not furnish them.[5]

Now, the federal army sweeps into a state. With no weapons for its militia, the state is helpless to resist. Indeed, even if the federal government had not emptied the armories, federal troops would merely need to capture these few buildings to preclude any resistance by the state militia. Or, if federal troops could secure general control of the state before many guns had been distributed from the central armories to the dispersed populace, they would not even need to capture these well-defended strongholds. In all of these scenarios, the whole able-bodied population of the state might well stand ready to defend the state against federal takeover. But when the militia is denied access to its arms, it is rendered impotent. Now assume, however, that the Constitution protects private gun ownership, and most people own the guns they use for militia service. A rapid disarmament of the state is no longer possible. Now, even if federal forces should topple the state government, thereby gaining nominal command of the militia, well-armed militia units can re-organize under local commanders and resist the federal invasion.

Hence, it is quite consistent to maintain that the framers' primary concern in drafting the Second Amendment was to ensure that the states always be able to form militias, and that they intended for this amendment to guarantee an individual right to bear arms. Whether or not the framers also intended to confer a collective right, by guaranteeing the individual right, they ensured the presence of empirical conditions under which states could always form well-armed militias. And this empirical possibility of raising a militia is what a state would really need if the federal government ever began tyrannizing over it—a tyrannical federal government will ignore any rights a state may have, anyway, so the state needs accessible guns to resist federal troops, not more abstract rights.

In terms of the test of tenability, therefore, interpreting the Second Amendment as guaranteeing an individual right to bear arms for militia service is a tenable reading of this amendment. Interpreting it as guaranteeing or conferring a collective right of states to form militias is much less tenable, given the amendment's language and the natural right doctrine it invokes. None of this diminishes the fact, however, that the framers' primary purpose in drafting the Second Amendment was to ensure that the states always be able to form militias, thus providing a check on the power of the federal government.

It should be noted that the interpretation of the Second Amendment advocated here does not imply an absolute and unlimited individual right to keep and bear arms. For one thing, the amendment's protection extends only to those arms that have some conceivable military application, and thus which could be of possible use in the context of militia service. Admittedly, distinguishing weapons that have a military use from those that do not is difficult in practice—a possible military use could probably be dreamed up for almost any weapon. Nevertheless, the theoretical distinction is important, for if the Second Amendment's purpose is to ensure that the states be able to form militias, then the amendment would not appear to protect gun ownership for, say, hunting. And as a practical matter, legislators and judges can use common sense to draw reasonable, if imperfect, lines between protected and unprotected guns.

Secondly, under this interpretation, the Second Amendment does not give citizens a right to form "unorganized militias" falling outside of government control, as is sometimes maintained. The Second Amendment's express purpose is to ensure the ability of states to form "well-regulated" militias, and an unorganized militia is precisely the opposite of this, by definition being subject to no governmental regulation. Hence, the federal government may legitimately ban the formation of private armies and restrict such related activities as the stockpiling of weapons.

Finally, while the Second Amendment, as interpreted here, protects individuals against federal restrictions on gun ownership, it provides no such protection against state or local restrictions. And this will continue to be the case until federal courts explicitly incorporate the Second Amendment into the Fourteenth. One may coherently argue that the Supreme Court should take this step. I will not make this argument here, however. Instead, I now turn to the question of whether it still makes good sense to constitutionally protect the right to bear arms at all.

America's Changing Political Culture

I have repeatedly stressed that when the Bill of Rights was drafted in 1789, the Second Amendment made excellent constitutional sense. Ensuring the ability of the states to form militias by guaranteeing an individual right to bear arms, the Second Amendment helped realize the purpose of the larger Constitution: erecting a system of government that would allow for effective governance, while structurally inhibiting the emergence of tyranny. As we enter the twenty-first century, Americans share their forebears' loathing of tyranny. But are the state militias still a necessary and appropriate institution for inhibiting the rise of tyranny? Does the Second Amendment right to bear arms still make good constitutional sense?

Up to 1763 and even beyond, most American colonists were content to be subjects of the British crown. In the 1780's, monarchy was still the accepted political system throughout Europe (though the king's days were numbered in France). Hence, when the framers of the

American Constitution set out to fashion a republic grounded on democratic principles, they were engaged in a daring experiment in government. Drawing on Locke and Montesquieu, their primary strategy for making the government effective yet resistant to tyranny involved spreading power out among multiple institutions and individuals, while establishing a system of checks and balances among the various governmental entities. Largely because the framers crafted such a brilliant system of government, the United States has enjoyed a political stability over the past 220 years unprecedented in the modern world. Over this period, a democratic culture has evolved, not just in the United States, but across Europe and in many other countries, some of which have adopted constitutions expressly modeled after the United States Constitution.

Hence, whereas in the 1780's, monarchy was the political norm in the West and a democratic republic a risky experiment, democracy is now the favored form of government across the developed world and dictatorship is shunned; the few surviving European monarchs now play only ceremonial roles. In no other country, however, has democratic culture come so close to attaining the status of a civic religion as in the United States. Americans treat their constitution as sacred writ, venerate the Founding Fathers as mythological sages, and revere as martyrs those who give up their lives in the cause of freedom. The Cold War only heightened the American ardor for democracy: the world was transformed into an apocalyptic battleground between the forces of democracy and communism, freedom and tyranny, good and evil. The slightest sympathy for socialist ideals was treated as blasphemy, and if the inquisition of heretics led to some undemocratic excesses—witness the McCarthy hearings—the driving factor was at least a genuine love of democracy. Nor has the fact that the United States has often failed to live up to its democratic ideals led to disillusionment with the ideals, themselves. On the contrary, civil rights leaders have championed the same democratic principles the framers sought to institutionalize in the Constitution, merely pointing out that these principles cannot be fully realized until they shape the lives of all Americans. Foreigners sometimes find curious the American attachment to certain patriotic rituals, such as the playing of the National Anthem before sporting events. To Americans, however, it is quite natural to pay frequent and sincere tribute to a country that was born of a struggle for liberty and continues to keep freedom alive.

All of this is simply to say that America's democratic institutions, together with the democratic culture these institutions have fostered, have rendered the threat of tyranny emerging in the United States far more remote today than it was two centuries ago. Whereas the attempted seizure of power by a would-be king was a real possibility for the framers, it is now difficult even to imagine a scenario by which any person or group within the federal government could accumulate enough power to warrant reaction by the state militias. How might such a situation develop? Assume a sitting president is voted out of office by a slim margin, amidst reports of widespread voting irregularities. The country, moreover, is in the middle of a war. Citing election fraud and national security considerations, the President declares he will not step down from office but remain in power as long as conditions warrant. How would Americans react to such a pronouncement?

Most likely, the President's closest advisors would try to get him committed to a mental institution, believing the strain of the job had caused his mind to snap. Certainly, no one in the political realm would dare voice the slightest support for the President's pronouncement—to do so would be to commit both treason and political suicide. Nor could the President hope for support from the federal police or military. Though undoubtedly loyal to their commander-in-chief, both officers and rank and file are typical American citizens, and they would be just as puzzled by the President's attempted coup as the rest of the country. Hence, any calls the President might make for troops to march down Pennsylvania Avenue to occupy the Capitol would be met with stunned inaction. If it appeared the President was actually sincere in his intent to remain in office, both houses of Congress would quickly convene to impeach the president and remove him from office, on charges of treason. The votes in both the House and Senate would be unanimous, no legislator wanting to go on record as voting to subvert democracy. If the President still refused to leave the White House, federal agents, acting on the Senate's verdict, would move in and arrest him. The country as a whole would be dumbfounded by the strange turn of events, but the overwhelming consensus would be that the president had lost his mind, and Congress had taken the only possible course in removing him from office. Americans will fight quite bitterly within the boundaries of their political system. Revering this system, however, they know its boundaries well and will uniformly condemn any attempts to overstep them. Most Americans would probably take up arms to defend their democratic system if it became necessary. But as the scenario just played out suggests, the system itself is so strong that events could scarcely reach a point where mass armed resistance was needed even in the unlikely event that elements within the federal government should try to establish a tyranny.

It might here be objected that the past century has witnessed numerous countries establishing democratic governments on roughly the American model, only to end up back in dictatorship when an elected official refuses to properly cede power or the military stages a coup. While this has certainly occurred, none of these countries have had democratic histories stretching as far back as that of the United States. On the contrary, most have had long traditions of colonial rule and dictatorship. Consequently, even when such countries adopt American democratic institutions, the culture remains more dictatorial than democratic in character, and people accept extralegal seizures of power as part of life, for this is how governments have always come into power. It is sometimes argued that developing countries are better off with benevolent dictators than democratic regimes, not yet having the cultural foundations upon which a stable democratic order could stand. Whether or not this is true, the fragility of very young democracies cannot be taken to imply that American democracy is equally fragile.

Nor is it appropriate, as is often done, to cite Hitler's quick rise to power in Germany as a warning of what could happen in the United States if Americans do not stand armed guard. When the Weimar Republic was established in 1919, Germany had never had a democratically elected government. Instead, most of the German principalities and dukedoms brought together by Bismarck in the 1860's had long histories of near-authoritarian rule, and many Germans blamed the disaster of World War I and the subsequent humiliation of the Treaty of Versailles on the directionless leadership of Kaiser Wilhelm II. Consequently, when Hitler, promising economic recovery in the face of hyperinflation and a return to German dominance, suspended the 15-year-old Weimar Constitution in 1934, he met with little opposition. In the 1930's, the United States was likewise in the throes of depression. Yet, with their deep-rooted sense of democratic values,

Americans never even toyed with the idea of setting aside constitutional freedoms to give the government greater powers to improve the economy. On the contrary, Americans rallied to the cause of fighting Hitler simply because he had proved himself an enemy of democracy and freedom. Hitler hoodwinked his fellow German citizens, who were inexperienced in democracy; he could not have won the support of many Americans, who are reverent of democracy.

Thus, for the United States, the threat of tyranny emerging is far more remote today than it was 200 years ago. Does that mean a future slide into tyranny is impossible? Of course not. Anything is possible, and none of us can claim to know the future. So would we not be wise to retain those constitutional and institutional safeguards that have proved so effective in preventing the rise of tyranny in America thus far? Common sense would indeed seem to dictate that you do not throw out something that has served you well in the past. On the other hand, times change. And while a constitution must take all necessary measures to ensure the preservation of the state, if it is to be lean, it cannot protect against every eventuality; it must focus on the most likely threats. By the same token, if a government is to be lean, it cannot maintain institutions to protect it against every conceivable danger, no matter how remote. The state must selectively organize its resources to combat the most likely dangers. The United States is undeniably much less threatened today by the possible emergence of tyranny than it was at its founding. This makes it legitimate to question whether constitutionally ensuring the ability of states to form militias still makes sense. Probably it would make sense to retain the state militias on the principle of "better safe than sorry"—if they still served as an effective check on federal tyranny. But this too may be questioned.

The Demise of the Militia

The first thing to note is that, whereas the state militia was a well-established and (mostly) well-respected institution in 1789, today there are no state militias, at least in the sense the framers understood. Early in the nineteenth century, the militias fell into serious decline. Musters were held once a year, if that, and these gatherings often involved more drunken carousing than drilling. Most militiamen handled firearms only on this annual occasion, and they were such notoriously bad shots that townspeople would come out to heckle their target practice sessions. In fact, after the Civil War, the National Rifle Association was set up to promote the sport of target shooting, with the express hope that this would keep Americans from slipping back into their dreadful pre-war marksmanship. As attempts were made in the second half of the nineteenth century to professionalize the state militias, they gradually evolved into the National Guard. The National Guard is a professional, non-conscript, part-time military service that falls under the dual command of the various state governors and the President. Units are charged with a variety of civil defense duties in their home states, and they may be called up by the President in times of national crisis.

While this attempt to professionalize the state militias was certainly successful, the irony is that the states were left without militias in the original sense, the National Guard being a professional military force the framers would have viewed as a standing army. Indeed, the only major difference between the National Guard and the other armed services is that its members serve part-time, while maintaining full-time civilian careers. Significantly, only a small percentage of the adult population serves in the National Guard, whereas the militia had traditionally been composed of all able-bodied males. Moreover, the federal government supplies the National Guard with all its weaponry; Guard members could not report for duty with privately owned weapons if they wanted to. At best, then, the framers would have regarded the National Guard as a "select militia," a variety of militia they trusted little more than the standing army, being composed only of citizens the government has selected and armed.

Nor would it be easy for a state government today to raise a militia of the traditional variety, composed of all able-bodied adults bearing their own weapons. At most, only about half of all American households own firearms, and fewer still own the long guns appropriate for militia service. A large number of American adults have never fired a gun in their lives. Hence, if the purpose of the Second Amendment was to ensure that the states be able to form militias, the amendment is now obsolete, since the states no longer have militias in the traditional sense.

The reply might be made that, if states do not currently have militias, they *should*. And if most citizens lack the requisite arms and shooting skills, perhaps the states could adopt the Swiss model and issue a rifle to every qualified man (or every qualified adult), while holding mandatory drills and target practice on weekends and holidays. It is unlikely any states will seriously consider taking this step, however, or that the federal government will encourage them to do so, for the state militias no longer play any role in America's national defense strategy. Remember that in England and colonial America, the militia's primary duty was always to defend the country against foreign invasion and domestic insurgency. Only secondarily did it serve as a check on the central government. Moreover, everyone agreed that professional armies make better fighting forces than militias, given their superior discipline and training, their standardized weaponry, and the greater willingness of professional soldiers to engage in long campaigns far from home. Indeed, most European countries maintained standing armies out of necessity, to keep from getting crushed by their neighbors. Only due to her island geography was England able to get away with relying on a militia for national defense. Some of the framers hoped the United States could similarly rely on the state militias for national defense, given America's relative isolation from Europe. But the young country found it still faced a number of threats on the American continent, including Britain, Spain, the Indians, and even its recent benefactor, France. Hence, delegates to the Constitutional Convention agreed they could not tie the hands of future governments facing unforeseen dangers by enacting such a constitutional ban. And, in fact, the federal army was never disbanded. Since its founding, the United States has always maintained a permanent, professional military. In 1800, the United States Army was composed of around 7000 men. Over the next 170 years, as the state militias fell into decline and disappeared, the federal military steadily grew until reaching a peacetime peak of about 3 million members in 1970, subsequently shrinking to the current level of around 1.5 million men and women.

That the United States came to rely on a professional federal military rather than the state militias for national defense was inevitable, for if hundreds of years ago standing armies were more effective than citizen militias from a military standpoint, this is far more true today, due primarily to advances in military technology. Whereas the foot soldier with a musket or rifle once formed the backbone of any military force, militia or professional army, developed nations now design their national defenses around such massive weapons systems as intercontinental ballistic missiles, aircraft carriers, jet fighters, tanks, and submarines. This weaponry is so complex that it simply could not be mastered by civilians practicing a few weekends a year—becoming a proficient fighter pilot or tank commander requires years of training. And with price tags in the hundreds of millions of dollars, no one suggests the traditional militia policy of "bring your own weapons" could ever be applied to tanks or planes. Indeed, this weaponry has such enormous destructive power that public safety demands it be kept in government control at all times. Hence, if citizens assembling with privately-owned muskets might once have composed a national defense force only slightly less effective than a standing army, today bands of citizens carrying their own rifles would constitute nothing resembling a modern professional military force. Switzerland is the exceptional case here, but she relies more on a centuries-old tradition of neutrality than on the rifles her citizens carry to protect her from attack. For a country as involved in global political and military affairs as United States, national defense needs have surpassed the capabilities of the citizen militia.

By the same token, the United States no longer relies on citizen militias to put down domestic insurgencies, this duty now being assigned to professional police forces and the National Guard. Nor would we want bands of armed civilians to be responsible for quelling civil unrest. When rioting does occur these days, charges of police brutality inevitably fly as officers trained in crowd control techniques use water cannons, tear gas, and rubber bullets to disperse rioters. Imagine what would happen if groups of relatively untrained civilians, carrying their own guns and live ammunition, were sent in to put down such riots.

Thus, in twenty-first century America, state militias of the traditional variety are no longer suited to fulfilling what had traditionally been their primary duty, defending against foreign invasion and domestic insurgency. Consequently, if a state were nevertheless to form a militia composed of every able-bodied adult, privately armed, the only role such a force could play would be the traditional secondary role of militias: checking the power of the central government. At best, this makes the case for raising state militias far less compelling than in former times. More strongly, there would seem to be something strange about a government maintaining an institution which had as its *sole* purpose checking the government's power by means of armed force. Certainly, the English crown never would have consented to the militia if it did not, first and foremost, anchor England's national defense and do so at much lower cost than a standing army. Would it be reasonable, then, to expect the federal government to permit, much less train and equip, state militias whose sole purpose it was to resist the federal government through armed force? And what would such training consist in, assuming the federal government was the only foreseen adversary? The best way to kill federal agents? How to sabotage US Army tanks? Maintaining the state militias on these terms would appear more likely to undermine democratic processes than strengthen them, by tempting states to veto unpopular federal decisions through the threat of armed revolt. Granted, militias have always had this latent power, though they have historically used it sparingly, turning against the government only in cases of direst oppression. In former times, however, the institutional focus of the militia was defending the country. If the entire *raison d'être* of the state militias is to check federal power, can we be confident they will be so restrained in their threat or use of force in the future?

Furthermore, even if state militias are retained for the sole purpose of checking the federal government's power, we must ask whether they can properly fulfill this role. The state militias are no longer relied on for national defense because advances in weapons technology have rendered them virtually impotent against the modern, professional militaries of other countries. Yet, the armed forces of the United States are the most advanced in the world, possessing armaments ranging from tanks to attack helicopters to nuclear missiles. Hence, as many commentators have pointed out, should the various branches of the federal government somehow conspire to oppress the people, and should they somehow convince the military to be the instrument of this oppression, there is very little bands of citizens carrying rifles could do to resist this onslaught. In seventeenth-century England or colonial America, a militia taking the field against the standing army stood on roughly equal terms with its adversary. The army might have had the advantage of better training and a few artillery pieces, but the militia could hope to assemble greater numbers and to fight with greater zeal, its members defending their homes or basic liberties. In any case, both the army and the militia would be predominantly composed of foot soldiers bearing the same type of weapon, so an approximate balance of power was ensured.

Developments in military technology over the past several hundred years have dramatically skewed this balance of power in favor of the professional army. This point may be driven home through an extreme example. Imagine the President issues an executive decree requiring that Oregonians begin paying a high tax on coffee shipped into their state. The Oregonians, outraged at this taxation without representation, take to the streets with hunting rifles and physically drive federal trade officials from their offices. The federal government responds by launching a nuclear missile strike against Portland. Without further protest, Oregonians submit to the coffee tax. Is it likely that the federal government would ever use nuclear weapons against its own citizens? Of course not. The point, however, is that whatever level of resistance a citizen militia might muster, the federal military can overwhelm it with far more destructive weaponry. Nor are the greater numbers of "the people" of much help anymore. In his famous defense of the militia in *Federalist Papers*, Madison calculates that the United States of his day could not support a standing army of more than thirty-five thousand soldiers. Such a force, Madison writes, would be no match for "a militia amounting to near half a million of citizens with arms in their hands."[6] Madison, however, assumes a rough parity in weaponry. His calculations break down when a hundred men armed with rifles prove to be little match for a single Abrams M1 tank.

Proponents of the militia will likely object that recent history offers numerous examples of lightly armed popular armies overcoming modern, professional armies by adopting guerilla tactics. Knowing they cannot beat the professional army on the open battlefield, the guerilla forces do not try to. Rather, they hole up in remote areas and harass the army, attacking by such unconventional methods as ambush, sabotage, and assassination. As the war drags on and casualties mount, the army may discover various other pressures building up against it, such as flagging troop morale, waning public support, intervention by outside countries, and international condemnation. Worn down by nagging attacks and frustrated by its inability to crush the rebels, the government may finally enter into talks with the guerillas, offering major concessions in exchange for peace. Or, if the army is a foreign invader, it may simply give up and go home. Such instances—Nicaragua, Angola, Vietnam, Afghanistan—prove that privately armed citizens banding together as unorganized militias can still influence events in the face of attack by modern, professional militaries.

This point is conceded. But two other points must be made. First, if a citizen militia may in some cases be able to hold off a professional army by adopting guerilla tactics, the militia's capacity for dissuading government tyranny is nevertheless much diminished from what it once was. The mere fact that the militia must resort to guerilla tactics rather than engaging in open battle demonstrates that the rough balance that used to exist between the militia and the standing army has become an extreme imbalance. This imbalance, moreover, promises to grow, for it stems primarily from advances in military technology, and this technology will keep developing, whereas there are limits to the firepower that can be incorporated into weapons suitable for private ownership. Hence, not only are the state militias no longer capable of playing their traditional primary role, but they have a much diminished capacity to fulfill their traditional secondary purpose, that of checking the power of the federal government by counterbalancing the federal military.

Second, in most recent cases of a guerilla movement achieving some sort of victory over a professional army, this has been because the professional army has held back, rather than unleashing all the destructive force it had at its disposal. In Vietnam, the United States waged—and lost—a limited war against the Viet Cong, dissuaded from raising troop levels or using its most destructive weaponry by a combination of domestic opposition to the war and fears of the war escalating into a global conflict. The Soviet Union was limited to using a fraction of its military power in Afghanistan by similar considerations, with the result being that the invasion stagnated, and the Mujihadeen ultimately outlasted the mighty Soviet Army. To cite some recent examples of governments holding back in conflicts with their own citizens, Great Britain has refrained from waging an all-out military campaign against Catholic militants in Northern Ireland, while the Mexican government has chosen to contain, rather than crush, the Zapatista uprising.

New Political Realities

Why do contemporary governments tend to hold back in guerilla conflicts, usually committing greater firepower to the conflict than the guerillas can muster, but refraining from using the massive force they have at their disposal to utterly destroy the rebel movement? Governments have come to realize they need legitimacy to govern effectively. And in large parts of the world—especially in the developed, western world—legitimacy is now acknowledged to come from the consent of the governed. In other words, contract theory has triumphed as the world's dominant account of legitimate authority. Hence, if a government uses massively disproportionate force to eradicate a sizeable resistance movement, it is obviously ruling by force, not consent. And this throws the government's legitimacy into question, thereby compromising its future ability to govern. To illustrate, assume a large contingent of rebels, upset at perceived abuses of government power, assembles in the mountains. In an open letter to the people, the rebels declare themselves unbound by government rule and proclaim their intention of toppling the government. No longer may the government claim to have legitimate authority over the rebels, since legitimacy comes from the consent of the governed, and the rebels have explicitly withdrawn their consent. Of course, the government may use force to suppress the rebels, the rebels themselves having opted out of civil society and declared war on the government. And since no rights or laws apply in the state of war other than the law of force, the government *could*—with no violation of law, either civil or natural—use the massive force at its disposal to utterly annihilate the rebel movement, including the civilians and even the whole communities that actively support it.

The government, however, must consider the long-term repercussions of taking such a heavy-handed approach. Once it eradicates all those who explicitly reject its rule, the government can hardly claim to enjoy the tacit consent of its remaining citizens. In the eyes of everyone concerned—the remaining citizens, individual members of the government and military, the international community—the remaining citizens will clearly have been intimidated into giving their consent. But forced consent is no consent, at all. Hence, the government will have lost its legitimacy. And in practical terms, this can seriously weaken a government. Among its own citizens, the government will never be able to win back the support of anyone who sympathized with the rebels even slightly. Even citizens who opposed the rebel cause may withdraw their support of the government, outraged at the government's excessive brutality, or suddenly fearful for their own liberties. Some of these disillusioned people may be members of the government or military—people especially well positioned to undermine government policy. Finally, a government practicing genocide will lose its legitimacy in the eyes of the international community, which can led to such unwelcome consequences as boycotts, trade sanctions, exclusion from international organizations, and even military intervention.

Thus, while any government facing a guerilla uprising must find it tempting to do something equivalent to firing a nuclear missile at Portland, this has become less and less of an option, at least in the developed world. As long as a government offers only a measured response to rebel attacks, it essentially declines to enter into a state of war with the rebels and rather uses its legitimate police powers to confront criminals violating the laws of the state. This approach is far from ideal for the government, for it may be dragged into a low-intensity conflict lasting years when it knows it could eradicate the rebels in days, and it may be forced to make unpleasant concessions to achieve peace. But at least the government cannot be accused of forcing the larger populace to consent to its rule. This allows the government to retain its legitimacy in the eyes of most concerned, thus dramatically increasing its future chances of being able to govern effectively.

What these considerations suggest is that when a band of guerillas uses small arms to wage war on government troops, the most powerful weapons they carry are not their rifles. For the government can always justify responding militarily to an armed uprising and can use greater firepower than the rebels can muster. If the rebels carry rifles, the army can fire back with machine guns. If the rebels get hold of machine guns, the government can justify using tanks to wipe out the machine gun nests. And if the rebels acquire rocket launchers to fire at the tanks, the government may start calling in air strikes against the rocket launchers. The government is held back, however, from unilaterally escalating too dramatically and simply eradicating the rebels, for this would compromise its long-term legitimacy. Consequently, the most powerful weapon the rebels carry is not their rifles. It is their withheld consent to government rule, by means of which they hold the government's legitimacy hostage. Withheld consent is such a powerful weapon because the government cannot counter it simply by escalating the military campaign. On the contrary, the government's need for consent is what limits its military response. Recognizing the unique properties and powers of withheld consent is crucial for the rebels, for they can properly utilize this weapon only when they know they hold it. And if the rebels wish to truly exploit their most powerful weapon, then rather than focusing on the military campaign—in which the government can always trump them with greater firepower—they are wiser to pour all their energies into making the statement, "We do not consent!" as loudly and firmly as possible.

New Modes of Resistance

In fact, resistance movements around the world have developed a number of highly vocal means of explicitly withholding their consent from a government without taking up arms, thereby robbing the government of its pretext for violent response. These methods include boycotts, strikes, civil disobedience, and perhaps most importantly, massive street demonstrations. When large masses of people refuse to purchase government products or services, shut down factories, and blockade major transportation corridors, they can bring the nation's economy to a standstill. Admittedly, the people themselves will feel the effects of such a standstill sooner than government officials, who typically have plenty of provisions tucked away in reserve. But the point is not to starve the government out of office. The point is rather to make an unambiguous, unmistakable statement that the people do not consent to the government's rule. And this proclamation is only made louder the more people begin to suffer economic deprivations, their perseverance in the face of hardship demonstrating the depth of their commitment. Nothing speaks more loudly, however, than hundreds of thousands of people taking to the streets, chanting, banging drums, blowing whistles, and carrying signs that proclaim, "We reject the government!"

Striking confirmation of the revolutionary power of mass demonstrations was provided by recent events in Eastern Europe. For years, the powerful East European armies, backed by the Soviet military, had quashed any meaningful resistance, armed or unarmed, to communist rule. The communist governments, incidentally, justified their rule through reference to the social contract: they claimed to be the true representatives of "the people," western governments being mere puppets of the capitalist class. But when the Soviet Union began to fall apart politically and economically, Marxist ideology was discredited, and the repressive governments of Eastern Europe lost any legitimacy they may have once had in the eyes of their people. Still, these governments were not about to give up power lightly. And though they could no longer rely on Soviet tanks rolling in, they retained plenty of troops and police of their own. Had the citizens of Eastern Europe been privately armed, perhaps they would have broken out in armed revolt. The governments would have responded militarily, and a bloodbath would have ensued, with unknown results. The communist governments, however, had not permitted private gun ownership, so the people knew they would have to use relatively non-violent means to overthrow their governments.

Hence, the peoples of Eastern Europe held general strikes, circulated anti-government literature, and defied government orders. Most importantly, they flocked to the main squares of the big cities and staged massive demonstrations, cheering on speakers who proclaimed the illegitimacy of the government. Night after night, people came back, sometimes under miserable weather conditions, proclaiming their non-consent. When police tried to forcibly shut down demonstrations, this only brought more people out to the streets. One by one, the East European governments began to crumble from within, the leaders recognizing the hopelessness of the situation. Perhaps they could have forestalled collapse by ordering military action against the demonstrators. But soldiers might have refused to fire on their fellow citizens, and in any case, this would have only put off the inevitable. So, one by one, the communist regimes gave up. Relatively little blood was shed. Czechoslovakia's political transformation was so peaceful it was dubbed the "Velvet Revolution." And because the new Czech government came to power through non-violent popular action, it enjoyed an instant legitimacy. The hundreds of thousands of people chanting in Wenceslaus Square made it clear to everyone at home and abroad that the old government had been overthrown and a new one instituted at the will of the people.

It was noted above that advances in military technology have been largely responsible for diminishing the ability of citizen militias to check the power of modern governments. But this does not mean free nations are therefore destined to collapse into tyranny, for other technological developments, especially in the field of communications, have greatly enhanced peoples' power to keep a check on their governments through non-violent means. Organizing a massive street protest must have been difficult—to say nothing about coordinating numerous protests around the country—when word could only be put out through hand-delivered pamphlets. Moreover, such protests could not hope to make much of a statement when newspapers were the only mass media outlet, and the government could easily take over the printing presses. But when a resistance movement sets up a telephone tree, a clandestine radio station, or a web site, the call for demonstrations can be put out to the whole country almost instantly. And when CNN broadcasts these demonstrations around the world, the government's attempts to hush up reports about them become laughable.

Indeed, in the American system of checks and balances, we could say the mass media have replaced the state militias as the peoples' most important check on the government, outside of voting. Yet, the media keep an even more vigorous watch on the government than did the militia. For whereas taking up arms was always a last resort option, to be invoked only when the government had already descended into tyranny, the media—in a ceaseless quest for "the scoop"—strive to shine a spotlight on government corruption at its first possible hint. The media, moreover, have a strong institutional interest in defending the Bill of Rights, and especially the First Amendment, since the freedoms of speech and press are what make the media industry possible. Advocates for the Second Amendment sometimes argue this amendment is what secures the First, since without the threat of armed resistance, the government might not let the media operate freely. Perhaps this was once the case. But you may ask yourself which you would prefer to brandish today if federal officials were unlawfully harassing you: a gun or a video camera? The first would get you shot by federal agents justifiably claiming self-defense, the second, a spot on the national news.

Does this mean the day of the armed rebellion is over, and tyrannical governments will henceforth be reformed or toppled only by less

violent means? Unfortunately not. In the developing world, especially, armed conflict will continue to be the most common method
of changing the form of government for the foreseeable future. This
is true of developing countries for several reasons. First, rather than
having traditions of rule by consent, developing countries typically
have traditions of rule by force, whether at the hands of colonial governments, army generals, or civilian dictators. People therefore tend
to accept whoever gains power as a matter of course, being unused to
demanding a government to which they consent. Second, with developing countries having less advanced militaries, rebel forces can often
achieve near-parity with the government army, especially if they can
secure military aid from foreign sources. And an armed uprising is
more likely to be launched if rebels believe they have some reasonable
hope for success. Thirdly, developing countries have more primitive
communications infrastructures than developed nations, thus making
it easier for the government to control mass communications, and
more difficult for rebels to utilize non-violent means of resistance.

Hence, many developing countries today occupy a situation similar to that which the United States occupied in 1789. A developing
nation drafting a constitution on democratic principles might therefore want to make constitutional provisions for a citizen militia, for
the same reasons the young United States enacted the Second
Amendment over two hundred years ago. But does it still make sense
for the mature United States to constitutionally ensure the ability of
states to form militias? The above arguments all suggest not; these
arguments may now be brought together.

Summation

When the United States was founded, Europe was ruled by kings, many
of them absolute monarchs. Having suffered under the tyranny of the
British crown and Parliament, the founders of the United States resolved to establish a republican government that would structurally
inhibit any possible rise of tyranny. To this end, the framers of the
American Constitution devised a system of government that separates
power among many different individuals and institutions, with each
government entity maintaining various checks and balances on the
others. To provide both the states and the people with a "last resort"

check against a potentially tyrannical federal government, the framers of the Bill of Rights constitutionally guaranteed the right of individuals to bear arms for militia service, so as to ensure the ability of states to form militias. This provision made excellent constitutional sense in 1789, for it helped define the structure of the notion's government, adding one more check to the system of checks and balances. Moreover, it proclaimed the political character of the United States as a republic that would not abide tyranny.

Over time, however, militias have lost their relevance in American society. For one thing, the need for such a "last resort" check on the federal government has diminished greatly over the last two centuries. The other democratic institutions the Constitution established and the democratic culture these institutions have fostered have both proved so strong that any attempts to subvert American democracy could scarcely get off the ground nowadays. And even if the federal government were somehow to move in the direction of tyranny, the state militias would not be the opposing force to stop it. No state today even has a militia in the sense understood by the framers. Nor can there be much argument for reviving the state militias. The traditional primary role of the militia was always to defend the nation against foreign invasion and domestic insurgency, but these days, professional military and police services must handle these duties. The military's current reliance on massive weapons systems simply makes it impracticable to transfer many of the military's duties to state militias composed of all able-bodied adults, arming themselves.

Yet, likewise diminished is the militia's ability to fulfill its traditional secondary responsibility, that of checking the power of the federal government by counterbalancing the federal military. In centuries past, parity of weaponry ensured a rough balance of power between the militia and professional military, thereby placing a check on the government's use of the military. Developments in military technology, however, have turned this former balance into a radical imbalance favoring the professional military. This may not render the militias completely powerless against the federal military, but it does mean citizen fighters could never hope to defeat the military on the open battlefield. All bands of armed citizens could do would be to adopt guerilla tactics and harass the federal troops, thereby proclaiming their non-consent to the government's rule. Yet, advances in communications technology now allow masses of people to make this statement far more effectively through largely non-violent means, including boycotts, strikes, civil disobedience, and street demonstrations. Not only do such methods lessen the bloodshed on both sides, but they enhance the protestors' legitimacy, since it is clear it is "the people" who are speaking, not just a small faction of armed men.

Any one of these considerations, taken by itself, would be enough to raise questions concerning the wisdom of retaining constitutional provisions designed to promote the institution of the state militia. Taken together, they argue strongly for the removal of these provisions. Quite simply, the country and the world have undergone changes that have rendered militias obsolete. The state militias helped the United States reach a point where even its future revolutions promise to be more "civil," so the militias occupy a proud place in American history. Having lost all relevance to contemporary American society, however, they no longer have place in the Constitution. Thus, on the principle that a strong constitution must be lean, containing only those provisions that materially help define a nation's political structure or character, I would argue that the Second Amendment should be repealed.

This argument assumes, however, that the Second Amendment merely guarantees individuals the right to keep and bear arms for purposes of militia service. Before this argument can be pressed, we must ask whether the framers might not have intended to guarantee an individual right that is not restricted to the militia context but is more or less unrestricted.

CHAPTER 7

The Unrestricted Right to Bear Arms

I have argued that the framers' primary concern in drafting the Second Amendment was to ensure that the states be able to form militias, to guard against federal tyranny, which they accomplished by guaranteeing an individual right to keep and bear arms for militia service. Yet, just because ensuring the viability of the militias was the framer's primary aim does not mean it was their only intent. They may have further intended to guarantee an individual right to bear arms for such purposes as hunting, target shooting, collecting, and self-defense; that is, they may have intended to guarantee an unrestricted individual right to bear arms.

In this chapter, I will assume the Second Amendment guarantees an individual right to bear arms, at least for purposes of militia service. The question now is whether the amendment's militia clause is limitative or not, that is, whether the amendment's opening clause limits the right to bear arms to the context of militia service, or whether it was intended simply to highlight the most important reason for guaranteeing the right to bear arms. Following the method introduced previously of testing proposed interpretations for tenability, I will ultimately argue that the militia clause should be read as limitative and hence that interpreting the Second Amendment as guaranteeing an unrestricted individual right to bear arms is not tenable.

The Intent of the Framers

The text of the Second Amendment, itself, does not make clear what function the framers intended the militia clause to perform. As gun advocates point out, whatever the clause's function, nothing in the Second Amendment's language or grammatical structure explicitly indicates that the militia clause limits the guarantee clause. Moreover, the fact that the Senate considered adding the phrase "for their common defense" to the guarantee clause but decided against it suggests the framers consciously held back from using the militia clause to limit the guarantee clause. Gun control proponents reply that if the militia clause is not read as limitative, then it would appear to have no legal import, whatsoever. Yet, the framers understood constitutions are no place to offer mere commentaries on the importance of certain institutions for the state; every constitutional provision should bear some legal weight.

One possible indication that the framers did mean to guarantee an unrestricted individual right is precisely the language they used of guaranteeing the right rather than conferring it. Again, this indicates they viewed the amendment as invoking a pre-existing natural right rather than conferring a new civic right. And Blackstone had established that the right to bear arms is a natural right derived from the natural right to self-defense. Thus, it may be argued, even if the framers were most concerned to ensure the ability of states to form militias, once they had guaranteed the individual right to bear arms for this purpose, it seems unlikely they would want to limit the constitutional protection for this right to the militia context. More likely, once they had invoked this natural right, they would go ahead and constitutionally guarantee the right to bear arms in its full, natural scope. After all, the right would continue to be in effect, anyway, as natural rights always are. So why not ensure that that the federal government completely and consistently recognize the right by granting it full constitutional protection? This line of reasoning is not definitive, but it supports the view that the framers intended to guarantee an unrestricted individual right to bear arms or at least an individual right to bear arms for any sort of self-defense, collective or individual.

Further support for this view can be gained by considering the historical backdrop against which the Second Amendment was written. In England, keeping a gun for defense of self, neighbor, and country had been a duty for centuries. People also used guns for hunting—at least when this was permitted, and sometimes when not—and other purposes. Hence, for most families, guns were simply a part of life, tools as ordinary and useful as hammers. And like most tools, guns have many uses. So if you had asked a seventeenth-century Englishman why he kept a gun, he would have vaguely called to mind all its possible uses, no more drawing a distinction between a gun kept for militia service and a gun kept for self-defense than we would distinguish between "hammers for driving in nails" and "hammers for prying out nails." Likewise in the American colonies, even when gun ownership was not required by law—which it often was—guns were essential tools for many people, especially in frontier areas. Consequently, it may be argued, when the framers considered the matter of private arms ownership, they would not have envisioned people keeping guns just for militia service. They would rather have assumed that people would use their guns in the usual way: as multi-purpose tools. Certainly, none of the framers would have suggested that if a man kept a gun in his house for militia service and an intruder broke in, he should not use the gun to defend his family. So it is unlikely the framers would have meant for the militia clause to be limitative, when they would not have conceived of people limiting their use of privately owned guns to any single purpose.

If this argument is persuasive, it is again not definitive. For one thing, the framers were intelligent men, and most were lawyers, so they certainly *could* have grasped the notion of protecting gun ownership for one use, but not for others. The English had already distinguished between the different uses of guns in their laws: for many years prior to passage of the Game Act of 1671, commoners were permitted to own guns for such purposes as self-defense and militia service but forbidden to use their guns for hunting. Furthermore, the muskets colonists were typically required to own for militia service were far less flexible than present-day rifles or handguns, so there are limits to the extent anyone could have viewed them as multi-purpose tools. With a loading time of several minutes—and no possibility of keeping a loaded gun in the house, since the powder would fail to fire after a few more minutes—muskets were hardly kept over the mantelpiece to protect against burglars. And eighteenth-century muskets were highly inaccurate, becoming militarily useful only when a whole company fired a volley together, so any colonist who took hunting seriously would buy a fowling piece or rifle; he would not rely on the musket he kept for militia service to put meat on the table.

Thus, neither the text of the Second Amendment nor the historical backdrop tells us definitively whether the framers intended for the militia clause to be limitative or not. Nor do the recorded debates or other documents from the period offer much help. Again, the Second Amendment received relatively little debate, and most of this focused on the conscientious objector clause, or more broadly on the importance of a militia for keeping the standing army in check. This could indicate the framers regarded the Second Amendment as purely a militia provision and thus that they intended for the militia clause to be limitative. Or it could mean everyone found it so obvious that an individual right to bear arms would be unrestricted that discussion of the point never came up. With little else to go on, if we are to reach any judgment on the tenability of interpreting the Second Amendment as guaranteeing an unrestricted individual right to bear arms, we can only ask whether it would have made good constitutional sense for the framers to guarantee such a right. Giving the framers credit, we may presume they did not draft any amendments that made bad constitutional sense. Or, if we are inevitably led to the conclusion that they did, this will be one further argument for repealing the Second Amendment.

The four primary reasons people own guns today are collecting, target shooting, hunting, and self-defense, with those who interpret the Second Amendment as guaranteeing an unrestricted individual right claiming the amendment protects gun ownership for all these purposes. The possible justification of a right to bear arms for self-defense differs significantly, however, from the justification that can be offered in the other cases, so it must be considered separately. I will first consider the possible right to keep and bear arms for purposes of collecting, target shooting, and hunting, labeling these "recreational" purposes, while acknowledging that hunting can be a person's source of sustenance. Later in the chapter, I will consider the possible right to bear arms for self-defense.

The Right to Bear Arms for Recreational Purposes

In 1789, the two primary reasons people owned guns were for militia service and self-defense. Still, many of the founder fathers were gun collectors, and with America's bountiful forests, hunting could be a source of income or pleasure for anyone who desired, not just wealthy landowners. Hence, although target shooting was not viewed as a sport until the second half of the nineteenth century, guns did have recreational uses when the Bill of Rights was drafted, so we may reasonably ask whether the framers intended to guarantee an individual right to bear arms for recreational purposes, as they would essentially be doing if they guaranteed an unrestricted individual right.

The first question to consider is whether the right to bear arms for recreational purposes is a natural right, as would be required for it to fit in with the Second Amendment's language. Fairly clearly, it is not. Natural rights are inalienable. The right to self-defense is a natural right, for even if I should profess to give up this right when I enter civil society, the state cannot hold me to my concession: if I am threatened with death and renege on my pledge not to defend myself, the state can try to hold me to my pledge only by threatening me with death, but it is because I fear death that I renege and defend myself. The right to take possession of material goods is similarly a natural right. Without a steady supply of material goods, I would die; hence, I cannot coherently give up my right to appropriate and consume those goods necessary for my survival any more than I can give up my right to self-defense. Yet, matters are different in the case of a particular type of material good, namely, guns kept for recreational purposes.

In the state of nature, I have the freedom to collect guns and shoot as many deer and targets as I like, just as I have the freedom to do anything within my power. Unlike the right to self-defense or to hold possessions generally, however, these freedoms are ones I may coherently give up when I enter civil society. Assume everyone entering into a particular society agrees to give up their freedom to own the shotguns they use to hunt ducks. The state can readily hold its citizens to this concession by policing them for shotgun possession and threatening violators with consequences worse than deprivation of one's shotgun, such as long jail sentences. Indeed, any sort of recreational activity, along with the requisite equipment, may coherently be given up when people enter civil society, since the state can meaningfully enforce the resulting bans. This does not mean entering civil society *requires* that people give up any particular forms of recreation, as it does require they give up their right to retribution. But it does mean a state may legitimately regulate the recreational activities of its citizens, there being no natural right to engage in any particular form of recreation or to own the requisite equipment, whether guns or golf clubs.

Although the language of the Second Amendment indicates the framers meant to invoke a natural right, we may ignore the amendment's language for a moment and ask whether it would have made good sense for the framers to constitutionally confer a civic right to bear arms for recreational purposes. For this to be a wise constitutional provision, it would have to somehow help shape the political structure or character of the nation. Yet, constitutionally protecting duck hunting and target shooting would obviously lend just about as much as much structure to the nation's political system as would protecting badminton or golf. Perhaps a slightly better case can be made for shooting sports helping to perpetuate the unique character of American society, which may be described as "freedom loving." Guns have frequently played a key role in America's ongoing quest for freedom, from the expulsion of the British to the push west by the pioneers to the defeat of Hitler. Thus, many sportsmen today say one of the reasons they like to collect and shoot guns is the link this gives them to the American past.

This particular attraction of gun ownership is granted. Nevertheless, one can celebrate the nation's heritage in many ways, from visiting the local history museum to staging historical reenactments to humming the national anthem at ballgames. And we would not want to provide constitutional protection for all these activities. Not only would this clutter up the Constitution with all sorts of provisions not properly constitutional, but it would restrict the government's legitimate power to regulate such "patriotic" activities, should any prove socially harmful. Suppose a group of Bostonians took to boarding British-registered ships once a year and tossing their cargo overboard, in memory of the Boston Tea Party. We would want the police to be able to halt this activity without having to worry about violating anyone's constitutional right to stage historical reenactments. Privately owned guns have the potential to cause much greater social harm than such tea parties, given that criminals can misuse guns that are intended for sport to intimidate or kill people. What sense would it make, then, to constitutionally rule out any possibility of restricting the ownership of such guns, no matter how much social harm their misuse might cause, merely to ensure that sportsmen could engage in a particular patriotic form of recreation?

This point needs to be made more strongly. Among recreational equipment, guns possess a unique lethality. Given this deadly power, it would contradict the very spirit of the social contract to constitutionally guarantee a right to own guns for recreational purposes. Assume that, for some reason, a certain type of shotgun used for duck hunting becomes the weapon of choice among armed robbers. Legislators must now decide whether the enjoyment many citizens get out of duck hunting is outweighed by the social evil being wrought by criminals making illegal use of shotguns. If the country has many duck hunters and few armed robbers, legislators will probably not take regulatory action. But if the crime wave surges, legislators simply must consider regulating shotgun ownership, to the point of banning it outright. After all, hanging in the balance is the ability of some people to enjoy a favorite pastime versus the lives of others. Granted, if a shotgun ban is enacted, criminals may still get hold of all the guns they need; legislators need to consider the practicality of gun restrictions before enacting them. Yet, a shotgun ban might be justified even if it made only a small dent in the number of people falling victim to shotgun-wielding criminals every year. Lives are at stake!

Now assume, however, that a constitutional provision prevents legislators from even considering the regulation of shotguns, no matter how many banks get robbed, no matter how many innocent victims get killed, and no matter how deep the state of fear into which the public sinks. Such a constitutional provision contradicts the social contract, for it ties the hands of a government attempting to respond to a public safety crisis, when people first left the state of nature and entered civil society precisely in order to attain greater security and escape from fear. Again, entering civil society does not require giving up one's shotgun or target pistols. But a government must be empowered to regulate this sort of recreational equipment when it threatens public safety, for mutually enhancing personal safety is the reason people invest the government with power in the first place.

This is an opportune point to address an objection gun owners commonly bring against any sort of gun control measures: regulating gun ownership punishes law-abiding citizens for the crimes of the guilty. In the scenario above, for example, a shotgun ban punishes law-abiding duck hunters for the actions of armed robbers. And this, the objection runs, is fundamentally unfair. In fact, an argument for constitutionally protecting gun ownership can be made on the grounds that gun control measures contradict the ideals of justice otherwise embodied in the Constitution, by punishing the innocent for the crimes of others. This objection, however, rests on a sloppy use of the term "to punish." In a very loose sense, "to punish" may mean, "to cause to suffer unpleasant consequences." And in this sense, the state could be said to punish gun owners by restricting their ownership privileges. In the same sense, however, bank robbers could be said to punish innocent bank employees when they shoot them in the course of their robberies. In debating a shotgun ban, therefore, we would have to decide which sort of "punishment" was more blatantly unfair.

Yet, the whole concept of punishment is out of place in this discussion. In a strict legal sense—the relevant sense here—punishment is retribution exacted against an offender for the commission of a crime. And gun bans, even if enacted in the wake of specific shootings, are not retributive measures. They are rather preventative measures, intended to keep guns out of the hands of those who might use them criminally. Necessarily, gun bans paint with a wide brush: the government cannot know beforehand who will use guns for criminal purposes, so it must make any such bans general. This means law-abiding gun owners may indeed suffer unpleasant consequences due to the actions of others. But the victims of gun crime also suffer because of criminal actions. Both types of suffering are social evils, and both are "unfair" in that innocent people suffer. It must be remembered, however, that it is the criminals who bring about this unhappy situation, not the government by taking measures to minimize the total social evil. Indeed, the government would only be act unfairly if, when weighing gun policy, it considered only the potential suffering of gun owners, and not that of gun victims. Yet, constitutionally protecting gun ownership for recreational purposes would essentially force the government to act in such an unfair manner, by preventing it from even considering restrictions on a certain type of recreational equipment, no matter how many people this equipment killed.

Likewise off track is the complaint that restrictions on gun ownership essentially place the blame for gun crime on law-abiding citizens, since it is only law-abiding citizens who respect gun bans, whereas criminals keep their guns. We should instead place the blame on criminals, it is insisted, and throw all our energies into prosecuting gun crimes, rather than taking guns away from law-abiding citizens. While raising an important point concerning the effectiveness of gun restrictions, this objection, insofar as it is an objection in principle to gun control, again rests on a sloppy use of language. No one "blames" law-abiding gun owners for the actions of criminals; everyone agrees criminals are responsible for their crimes, and they should be caught and punished. But when a society is wracked by gun violence, the case can be made that cracking down on criminals is not enough—the number of guns falling into criminal hands must also be reduced. Whether gun control measures effectively reduce the number of guns in criminal hands is an empirical question; it must be debated on the basis of whatever empirical data can be gathered. But what *would* be blameworthy on the part of law-abiding sportsmen would be if empirical data could be produced clearly showing that gun restrictions significantly reduce gun violence, yet sportsmen clung to their ownership privileges out of sheer love of their sport. Granted, in this case, the law-abiding duck hunter still does not threaten anyone with the shotgun he owns. Nevertheless, by insisting on his privilege of owning a gun in the face of such data, he shares, not blame for murder, but some responsibility for the additional deaths that occur as a result of the policy of legal gun ownership. Again, whether such data supporting the effectiveness of gun control measures can be produced is an empirical question; I do not make any such empirical claims here. The point here is that, if one advocates a *constitutional right* to own guns for recreational purposes, one is essentially insisting that the ownership of sporting guns be left unrestricted *even if a direct link should be established between legal gun ownership and increased gun violence.* And this is to insist that one's own ability to go duck hunting is more important than keeping other people alive. I would maintain that such a stance not only contradicts the social contract but is morally repugnant.

The text of the Second Amendment does not make clear whether the framers meant to invoke a right to bear arms for recreational purposes. Yet, because this putative right is not a natural right, and it would make such poor sense as a constitutionally conferred civic right, I believe we can assume the framers did not intend to either guarantee or confer an individual right to bear arms for recreational purposes. This implies the framers did not intend to guarantee a completely unrestricted individual right to bear arms. They must, therefore, have viewed the militia clause as limitative, at least to some extent.

It might be responded, however, that any gun owned for recreational purposes—or for any purpose, for that matter—can also be used for self-defense. And a better case can be made for the framers intending to guarantee an individual right to bear arms for self-defense. If this was the framers' intent, then the Second Amendment will presumably protect the ownership of any gun that can possibly be used for self-defense, whatever other uses it might have. This possibility will now be examined. Incidentally, for purposes of analysis, hunting may be considered a form of self-defense when it is a person's essential source of sustenance.

Is the Right to Bear Arms for Self-Defense a Natural Right?

A better case can be made for the framers intending to guarantee a right to bear arms for self-defense because a stronger case can be made for this right being a natural right. Again, Blackstone had derived the right to bear arms directly from the natural right to self-defense: we have a natural right to defend our lives, so we must have the right to equip ourselves for this purpose. The fact that Blackstone's *Commentaries* was the standard legal reference of the day, and that the framers used language to guarantee the right to bear arms, rather than confer it, strongly suggests they had Blackstone in mind when drafting the Second Amendment. But does this prove the framers intended to extend the right to bear arms beyond the context of militia service, to cover personal self-defense? No. After all, the Second Amendment makes no mention of self-defense, whereas it explicitly invokes the institution of the militia. And the debate surrounding the amendment's ratification focused almost exclusively on the collective self-defense of the states, not on individual self-defense. Given the ambiguity of the textual and historical evidence, ruling on tenability will again require considering for ourselves whether enacting a constitutional amendment that guarantees or confers an individual right to bear arms for self-defense would have made good constitutional sense in 1789. And the first question this brings up is whether the right to bear arms for self-defense is truly a natural right.

Before attempting an analytic response to this question, let us consider the historical reply. The right to bear arms originated in England, and we have already seen that—Blackstone notwithstanding—the English tradition hardly treated the right to bear arms as an inalienable natural right. This right made its first appearance in English law with the Bill of Rights of 1689. Prior to this, keeping arms had been a duty in England for hundreds of years, until the mid-seventeenth century when it became a privilege extended only to those "well-affected" toward the government, generally meaning Protestants. The Game Act of 1671 further limited the privilege of owning guns to the landed gentry. The Bill of Rights then transformed this privilege into a right. The Bill of Rights did not, however, overturn the Game Act. Beyond explicitly withholding constitutional protection from non-Protestants, Article 6 states that people "may have arms for their defense suitable to their condition and as allowed by law." This guaranteed ownership rights only for those of suitable condition—the gentry—while allowing this same gentry to decide who else could own guns "as allowed by law." If Parliament—composed of gentry—thought arming the commoners would be useful in its perpetual power struggle with the crown, it could broaden ownership rights. But if the gentry thought their tenants posed a greater threat, landowners could always disarm their tenants, using their authority as justices of the peace. Historically, therefore, the English did not treat the right to bear arms as an inalienable natural right, enjoyed by all people at all times. The right rather developed as a tool the English gentry wielded in its two-front confrontation with the king and commoners. Of course, the fact that the right to bear arms had such an undemocratic history does not mean it cannot be a natural right. The right may always have been in effect in England, though it took the English a long time to recognize it. Nevertheless, the right's curious genesis must give us pause before we to deem it one of those "truths we hold to be self-evident." Clearly, the right to bear arms was not always so self-evident.

Shifting now to a theoretical analysis of whether the right to bear arms for self-defense is a natural right, the question at hand can be made quite clear by referring back to Locke. If I am walking down the road and someone attacks me, Locke maintains, I may defend myself, whether I occupy the state of nature or civil society. This right to self-defense is a natural right I cannot coherently give up when I enter civil society, the state having no means of holding me to such a concession. If I occupy the state of nature and I survive the attack, I may personally hunt down my attacker and exact whatever retribution I see fit. But when I enter civil society, I give up this right of retribution, transferring it to the state. Now I must allow the proper authorities to apprehend and punish my attacker. Locke takes us this far. The question now is, prior to any specific attack, do I have a natural right to carry a weapon in anticipation of possible attack, such that I may be equipped to defend myself in this eventuality? Or is my freedom to carry a gun for self-defense one of those natural freedoms I enjoy in the state of nature, but which I may coherently give up on entering civil society?

Although Blackstone deemed the right to bear arms for self-defense an inalienable natural right, there would appear to be no incoherence to my giving up this natural freedom provided everyone else does likewise. For the state can readily hold us to our mutual pledge not to keep guns for self-defense: police can watch out for people carrying guns, and the courts can mete out punishments for illegal gun possession more unpleasant than deprivation of one's gun, such as long jail sentences. Granted, the state cannot threaten people with anything that would be worse than death at the hands of an attacker. But in most social contexts, the chances of falling victim to a lethal attack will be fairly remote, whereas the chances of getting caught illegally carrying a gun will be fairly high. So the state can meaningfully deter illegal gun possession. And this means we can coherently give up our natural freedom to own guns.

Indeed, it will be quite rational for us to collectively give up this freedom if we believe our chances of falling victim to deadly attack will be lower in a society where no one carries a gun than in a well-armed society. Of course, before I give up my gun, I must consider whether I can trust everyone else to carry through on their pledge to do likewise and whether I can trust the state to vigorously enforce gun possession laws. These are empirical questions that depend on such factors as the character of my fellow citizens, the structure and effectiveness of our government, and the quality of the police force. In principle, however, relinquishing my freedom to carry a gun, assuming everyone else does likewise, follows exactly the pattern of the larger social contract: each of us gives up a freedom we enjoy in the state of nature in the interest of enhancing our mutual security. Hence, the right to bear arms for self-defense is not a natural right derivable from the right to self-defense, for while the right to self-defense is inalienable, the right to bear arms may be coherently forfeited when we enter civil society. Civil society does not require that everyone give up this freedom, as is the case with the right of retribution. But a particular society may legitimately restrict the freedom to bear arms for purposes of self-defense, without violating anyone's natural rights.

Perhaps the following objection will be raised here. Assume I agree to give up my natural freedom to carry a gun, believing this will reduce my chances of falling victim to a deadly attack. Then, one day, I am waylaid by an attacker wielding a large knife. Had I been carrying a gun, I could have fended off the attacker. As it is, I am killed. In previously giving up my freedom to carry a gun, therefore, did I not forfeit my right to self-defense, since without a gun I was unable to properly defend myself? I did not. At the time I forfeited my right to carry a gun, I had no specific foreknowledge of the attack that was to take place. Had I somehow known I would be subject to an attack where only a gun could save me, it would have been irrational for me to give up my freedom to carry a gun. Or, even if I had professed to give up this freedom, it would have been irrational for me to keep my word, since even if I had been caught illegally carrying a gun, the state could have done nothing worse to me than what I knew my attacker was planning. But none of us have such specific foreknowledge of future events. All we can do is estimate the odds of encountering various threats under various conditions, such as falling victim to deadly attack in societies with and without legal gun possession. If we collectively estimate our chances of survival to be better in a society that restricts gun ownership, it will be irrational—contrary to our natural right to self-defense—to retain our natural freedom to carry guns. Even I should give up my freedom to carry a gun, then be killed by a knife-wielding assailant, I will still have made the most intelligent decision if the larger society experiences fewer total lethal attacks than it would have otherwise, for I have done what I could to maximize my odds of survival. Besides, who knows whether my attacker would have wielded a knife had guns been legal? Perhaps he would have carried a gun and shot me anyway. In any case, giving up my freedom to bear arms does not amount to a forfeiture of my natural right of self-defense. In some social contexts, it may well be my wisest exercise of this right.

Hence, the right to bear arms for self-defense is not a natural right. As such, it cannot be constitutionally guaranteed. If the framers intended to guarantee a right to bear arms for self-defense, they committed the theoretical error of guaranteeing a right that can only be conferred. Before considering the implications of this possible theoretical error, however, let us ignore the Second Amendment's language for a moment and ask whether it would have made good sense for the framers to constitutionally confer a civic right to bear arms for self-defense.

Gunland and Controlland

To address the question just posed, it will be helpful to construct a fic-titious scenario involving the nation of Constitutionia. Constitutionia is a federal republic composed of two states, Gunland and Controlland, each of which has 1 million residents. The country has a federal con-stitution very much like that of the United States, except that its bill of rights makes no mention of any right to bear arms. By statutory law, Gunland allows all competent adults to own guns and in fact en-courages gun ownership for self-defense. Controlland prohibits all pri-vate ownership of firearms, again by statutory law. Fortunately for us, both states are filled with accountants and scholars, so reliable statis-tics are kept on every aspect of public life, including gun violence.

In the year 2000, Gunland registered the following statistics:

- 80% of adults owned guns.
- 1000 attacks involving a gun took place.
- In 800 of these attacks, the victim also had a gun; these attacks resulted in 100 victims being killed, and 100 attackers killed.
- In the 200 attacks where the victim had no gun, 50 victims were killed but no attackers.

Hence, for the year, Gunland witnessed 1000 attacks, 150 victims killed, and 100 attackers killed. The public "fear level" in Gunland was rated low, each person having a mere 1 in 1000 chance of being attacked, and 85% of victims surviving their attacks. Moreover, because one's actual chances of surviving an attack went from 75% to 86% when one did carry a gun, people felt like they had some control over their personal safety.

The situation in Controlland was grimmer that year. Although Controlland prohibits gun possession, some guns do make their way across the border from Gunland, and criminals clearly viewed the unarmed citizens of Controlland as sitting ducks compared to their armed neighbors in Controlland. The following statistics resulted:

- 5% of adults owned guns.
- 2000 attacks involving a gun took place.
- In 100 of these attacks, the victim also had a gun; these attacks resulted in 12 victims being killed, and 12 attackers killed.
- In the 1900 attacks where the victim had no gun, 475 victims were killed but no attackers.

Hence, the year-end totals for Controlland were 2000 attacks, 487 victims dead, and 12 attackers killed. This was twice as many attacks as Gunland witnessed, with over three times the number of victims killed. The public fear level was rated high, people having a 1 in 500 chance of being attacked, and only a 76% chance of surviving such an attack. Moreover, because Controllanders could not buy guns to defend themselves, many felt helpless.

Clearly, it looks like Gunland adopted the wiser policy in 2000. Over the next decade, however, a number of gradual but profound changes took place in both states. In Gunland, with so many people buying guns, manufacturers flooded the market with cheaper models. The fear level being low, law enforcement was lax, and in this permissive environment, an illegal drug trade emerged. Drug dealers began routinely using guns against one another, police, and anyone else who got in the way, while junkies turned to armed robbery to support their habits. As a result, the statistics for the year 2010 were as follows:

- 90% of adults owned guns.
- 2000 attacks involving a gun took place.
- In 1800 of these attacks, the victim also had a gun; these attacks resulted in 225 victims being killed, and 225 attackers killed.
- In the 200 attacks where the victim had no gun, 50 victims were killed but no attackers.

Hence, the totals were 2000 attacks, 275 victims dead, and 225 attackers killed. The fear level was rated moderately high, with each
person having a 1 in 500 chance of being attacked, though 86% of
victims did survive their attacks. Most troubling, however, was the
275% increase in the number of victims killed from a decade previous.

In Controlland, meanwhile, police cracked down on both illegal
gun ownership and gun smuggling. With the fear level being high,
more police were put on the street; gun-related offenses were punished
severely and a public awareness campaign was conducted to teach
people how to avoid attack. Controlland's unarmed citizens were still
attractive targets for attackers, but the harsh sentences for gun possession, and even harsher sentences for using a firearm in the commission of a crime, helped deter some gun crime. A drug trade did develop
in Controlland, but the already-heightened police presence kept it
fairly limited. Controlland's 2010 numbers showed:

- 2% of adults owned guns.
- 1000 attacks involving a gun took place.
- In 20 of these attacks, the victim also had a gun; these attacks resulted in 2
  victims being killed, and 2 attackers killed.
- In the 980 attacks where the victim had no gun, 245 victims were killed but
  no attackers.

Hence, the totals: 1000 attacks, 247 victims killed, and 2 attackers
dead. This was half the number of attacks recorded in Gunland, and
10% fewer victim fatalities. The fear level in Controlland was still
moderate: the chances of being attacked had fallen to 1 in 1000, but
victims survived only 75% of their attacks, and still had no option of
arming themselves. Nevertheless, the number of victims killed had
been cut nearly in half over the course of the decade, even as victim
fatalities skyrocketed in Gunland. Consequently, though not yet satis-
fied with the situation, Controllanders believed their state to be on the
right path.

What is the point of this story? Not that gun control is necessarily a better policy than legal gun ownership. No fictitious scenario
could demonstrate this, especially using such contrived statistics.
Rather, the story illustrates that a state may take one of two basic
approaches to gun violence. It can permit, encourage, or even require
private gun ownership, on the reasoning that criminals will be deterred
from all sorts of crime by the fear of encountering armed victims. Or

the government can ban gun ownership so as to reduce the total number of guns in circulation, in hopes of decreasing the number of guns that fall into criminal hands. Of course, a whole spectrum of possible measures lies between these two approaches, such as permitting gun ownership but requiring registration. Still, the two basic approaches of legal gun ownership and restricted ownership are the poles that ground the spectrum of options between them. The story of Constitutionia further suggests that in some social settings, an approach leaning more toward one end of the spectrum will work better, whereas in other contexts, the opposite approach may prove more effective. What works for one state may not work for another, and policies that prove effective at one time may become outdated as a society changes. In any case, which approach will work better in any particular social setting is an empirical question, not a matter of principle. One may claim to support gun privileges or gun control "on principle," but no one can know how a particular approach will work until it is tried. Consequently, in attempting to reduce gun violence, all policy makers can do is look at past empirical data, try to take into account all the relevant factors in the present situation, and use their best judgment to settle on the approach they believe will have the greatest likelihood of success.

To get to the real point of the story, however, suppose that in 2010 Constitutionia were to enact a federal constitutional amendment conferring an individual right to bear arms for purposes of self-defense. Now, even if it wanted to, Gunland could not copy Controlland's relatively successful approach to gun violence. Just the opposite, Controlland would be forced to allow private gun ownership, thus likely reversing its recent decline in gun deaths and putting it on the same path toward escalating gun violence as Gunland. Or suppose the amendment had been enacted in 2000. Controlland never could have attempted its approach of maintaining gun controls, while cracking down on criminals. So the question is this: given that a government has two basic options for combating gun violence, with it being an empirical question which will work better in any particular situation, what could be the possible sense in constitutionally tying the government's hands, such that it can exercise only one of its two basic options?

Leaving Constitutionia and returning to the United States, the framers of the Bill of Rights never would have thought to enact an amendment constitutionally *prohibiting* private gun ownership. With so many Americans still inhabiting a frontier environment where guns were a virtual necessity of life, this would have contradicted the social contract by diminishing public safety and increasing the fearfulness of frontier dwellers. Yet, what more sense would it have made to enact an amendment *ensuring* legal gun ownership when the framers could not have know what sort of changes might take place in American society and thus whether enacting gun controls might not at some point be the best strategy for promoting public safety? This, too, would have contradicted the social contract, by constitutionally preventing future governments from taking steps which might, in some cases, be judged most reasonable toward ensuring public safety. Could the framers have wanted to do this? They wisely decided not to constitutionally ban standing armies in peacetime, unwilling to tie the hands of future governments facing unforeseen threats to national security. By the same token, it seems unlikely they would have wanted to tie the hands of future governments facing unforeseen threats to public safety by constitutionally depriving the government of half its possible policy options.

Guns and the American Character

Given that a constitutionally conferred right to bear arms for self-defense would contradict the very social contract, if one nevertheless wants to interpret the Second Amendment as conferring this right, one must show that it enshrines some value or principle so central to American society as to outweigh the right's negative effects. What such a value could be is hard to imagine. It is not enough to say, "We should be free to own guns because we live in a free state. *Freedom* is the value proclaimed by the right to bear arms." The term "free state" is composed of two terms, "free" and "state." If a state is to be free, it must indeed ensure some individual freedoms. But if it is to be a state, individuals must give up some of the freedoms they would otherwise enjoy in the state of nature. Some rights are inalienable; they can never be given up. All other freedoms are placed on the table when people enter civil society. A particular society may decide to enshrine certain natural freedoms as constitutional rights, even though they are not inalienable natural rights, because these freedoms somehow positively shape the political structure or character of the society. But to merit such special protection, a *particular* natural freedom must embody some *particular* value or principle fundamental to the society; the fact that it is a natural freedom is not enough to justify constitutional protection, since many such freedoms are given up when civil society is formed. In the state of nature, we have a natural freedom to carry guns for self-defense. But if one were to claim this freedom should be constitutionally protected simply because we are free, one could just as well argue our natural freedom to own hula hoops or nuclear devices should be constitutionally protected, again because we are free.

Perhaps it will be noted that America has a frontier heritage, and guns were an essential part of life on the frontier. Indeed, going back farther to America's English roots, there was the longstanding duty in England to keep and bear arms for defense of self, neighbor, and country. Guns are consequently a part of the American legacy. And this is a living legacy, since it has been passed down from parent to child for generations, especially in rural areas. Restricting gun ownership therefore cuts America off from her heritage, while disrupting a venerable cultural tradition. These threats to American culture alone justify constitutional protection for gun ownership.

To this it must be replied, first, that if many American families and communities have gun-owning traditions, others do not, particularly in urban areas. And while rural Americans may regard guns as cherished tools, city dwellers tend to associate guns with violence and murder. Naturally, rural folk resent it when city dwellers try to impose their urban values on the entire country, and gun control measures are seen as one of the worst of these impositions. Yet, open-minded rural residents will appreciate why city dwellers often take a different view of guns and why they often want to restrict gun ownership. With Americans splitting into two basic camps on the gun issue, roughly along urban-rural lines, all we can do is hash out the issue in the usual democratic fashion: in the legislative arena, with both sides putting forth their best arguments, perhaps offering some compromises, and finally trying to secure the most votes. To give a constitutional advantage to one side in this democratic struggle would make no more sense than constitutionally favoring the other.

As far as cutting America off from her cultural roots, it has already been noted that national heritage can be celebrated in many ways but that cultural activities do not, as a rule, merit constitutional protection. Moreover, if a culture is to remain vibrant, it must allow itself to evolve. On the American frontier, as in early England, there were no professional police forces. Consequently, people *had* to take primary responsibility for defending themselves, and justice *had* to be largely vigilante justice. Today, every corner of the United States has a well-established criminal justice system. Whether police are capable of protecting the populace, or whether privately owned guns are needed to deter crime, may be debated—indeed, this is the central question of the gun debate. But if empirical conditions once clearly demanded that private gun ownership be allowed, the question is now much more open. To forego this debate simply because we want to keep our cultural heritage alive risks committing us to policies that were crafted over two hundred years ago, based on the conditions of that earlier time, without any consideration for whether these policies still make good sense today.

In the end, I suspect the value many people see enshrined in the Second Amendment, interpreted as conferring an individual right to bear arms for self-defense, is that of "rugged individualism." We picture the hunter wearing skins, the farmer leading his family west, or the battle-hardened GI returning from Europe. As he carefully cleans his gun, he says, "No, I don't need the police to protect me and my family. I look after my own." Indeed, while any democracy must respect the integrity of the individual, the United States, more than any other nation, has come to regard individualism as a sacred value. From embracing the free market to rejecting universalized health care to limiting welfare benefits, Americans proclaim that, in our country, individuals not only must take care of themselves, but they can. Many would argue that this ethic of individualism is what lies at the heart of America's greatness. And, in many ways, this is no doubt true. Yet, in ancient Greek tragedy, the quality that makes a character great often turns out to be his tragic flaw—what ultimately brings about his downfall. Individualism could turn out to be the American tragic flaw. It could turn out to be our tragic flaw, if it causes us to forget that living in a free society does not mean protecting every conceivable freedom but sometimes giving up our individual freedoms for the collective good. If it blinds us to the fact that sometimes we are better off entrusting our security to the larger society, rather than relying on ourselves. If it leads us to view "the government" as an adversarial force bent on oppressing the people, when in fact we have strong democratic institutions to ensure that our government is literally by, of, and for the people.

Would you still insist on the absolute value of rugged individualism? Then let me ask you a question. You say you can take care of your own—at least, as long as you are allowed to own a gun. Yet, as your children grow up, there will be times you cannot accompany them, though they will not yet be old enough to carry guns themselves. What if I were to show you reliable statistics clearly demonstrating your child to be twice as likely to fall victim to a deadly gun attack in a community that permits gun possession than in a community with strict gun controls? Would you still insist on your right to own a gun? Yes, your sense of individualism is important. And yes, you feel safer and more in control when you carry a gun, instead of relying on the police for your protection. But do these comforting feelings justify subjecting your child to a greater risk of deadly assault? Perhaps you will reply, "You can't produce statistics like that. All the statistics I've seen show my kid to be safer in gun-owning communities." Maybe that is true. Maybe strict gun restrictions would be bad public policy today. But you cannot know how American society will develop over the next 25 years. When your grandchildren start growing up, social conditions may have changed to where gun control is undeniably the more effective public safety strategy. So do you really want to hamstring future policy makers as they attempt to craft laws that will better protect your grandchildren? If you insist, not merely on statutory laws that permit gun ownership but on constitutional protection for gun possession, you indicate a willingness to sacrifice future generations to gun violence in the interest of ensuring your own gun ownership privileges.

The Proper Forum for the Gun Debate: Statutory Law

Hence, a constitutionally conferred civic right to bear arms for self-defense would make no sense. The question of how a society can best ensure public safety is simply too dependent on changing empirical conditions for it to be a proper subject of constitutional law. By this same token, however, the gun issue's empirical basis makes it ideally suited to statutory treatment, statutory laws possessing both the flexibility and sensitivity to real-world details that constitutional laws lack. The appropriateness of the statutory forum for crafting gun policy was recently illustrated when Austrian gun manufacturer Glock developed a semiautomatic pistol built largely out of plastic parts, thereby raising the possibility of a gun invisible to airport security systems. While these "plastic guns" posed an obvious threat to public safety, it would have been unrealistic to ban all guns containing plastic parts, since many commonly owned and readily detectable handguns fall into this class. A compromise was therefore struck, and federal legislation was passed requiring all guns sold or possessed in the United States to contain the metal equivalent of at least 3.7 ounces of stainless steel—enough to trip the average metal detector.

Had federal courts recognized an individual right to own any gun that could be used for self-defense, presumably no laws could have been passed regulating plastic guns, thus leaving airlines exposed to frequent highjackings. Or, in any case, a constitutional amendment would have to have been ratified to exempt plastic guns from Second Amendment protection. This is certainly a cumbersome way to enact public policy. Moreover, incorporating such everyday details as the amount of metal guns must contain into the Constitution would significantly weaken the Constitution—it would quickly balloon to an unmanageable size and require amendment every time a new generation of metal detectors came out. As it is, federal courts have not interpreted the Second Amendment as guaranteeing or conferring an individual right to bear arms for self-defense, so statutory action was possible on plastic guns. A reasonable, targeted law enjoying broad support was crafted fairly quickly in response to a sudden technological innovation, and presumably this law can be updated with relative ease should further innovations take place in either the gun or security industries. The statutory process worked, and public safety was enhanced.

Should we give up the freedom we enjoy in the state of nature to keep and bear arms for self-defense or for recreational purposes? Not necessarily and not simply as a matter of principle. A constitutional ban on private gun ownership would make no more sense than a constitutional guarantee of such a right. After all, many law-abiding citizens own guns for purposes of collecting, target shooting, hunting, and self-defense, and there can be no reason to take away their guns if no social good is accomplished thereby. Indeed, gun advocates maintain that imposing gun restrictions will increase the social evil of gun violence—in the words of the National Rifle Association, "If guns are outlawed, only the outlaws will have guns." This argument no doubt has something to it, and it needs to be heard in the public policy debate on guns. But there is also something to the argument that decreasing the number of guns in circulation should decrease the number of guns that fall into criminal hands. I do not propose to enter into this public policy debate here. I want to insist, however, that *the proper forum for this debate is the arena of statutory law, not constitutional law.* For one thing, the gun issue's dependence on changing empirical conditions makes it far better suited to treatment by statutory than constitutional law. More importantly, tying the hands of future policy makers by constitutionally barring them from taking one of the two possible approaches to the problem of gun violence—without any consideration for the changing empirical circumstances that determine which approach will be more effective—would be both irrational and immoral.

The framers of the Second Amendment could not have foreseen whether broad gun privileges or tight gun controls would be the better strategy for promoting public safety in the United States two hundred years into the future. I would guess they realized this and thus did not intend to confer an individual right to bear arms for self-defense. This would mean they intended for the militia clause to be limitative and for the right to bear arms to extend only as far as militia service requires. If, however, the framers of the Second Amendment did intend to invoke an individual right to bear arms for self-defense, this was one of their few mistakes. If they followed Blackstone in believing the right to bear arms to be an inalienable natural right, they made a theoretical mistake. Or if they intended to constitutionally confer an individual right to bear arms for self-defense, they used poor judgment in crafting an amendment that made bad constitutional sense in 1789 and makes bad constitutional sense today. In any case, the arguments put forward in the last chapter for repeal of the Second Amendment still stand; indeed, they have been strengthened. All of the arguments advanced to this point may now be drawn together.

CHAPTER 8

Concluding Arguments

I have argued that the Second Amendment is best interpreted as guaranteeing an individual right to bear arms, though a right restricted to the context of militia service. Although this amendment was good constitutional law in its time, we would now be wise to repeal it, both because the amendment has become as obsolete as the state militias and because it disrupts the urgent public policy debate on guns.

The Antiquated Right

For a constitution to be strong, it must be lean. That is, it must contain relatively few provisions, but each of these should pack a punch, in some way shaping the fundamental political structure or character of the state. Because constitutional laws proclaim the enduring principles and values intended to guide the state over time, they need to be protected against shifting political winds. Thus, while a constitution will normally make provisions for its own amendment, this process should be more difficult than that of enacting statutory laws. Statutory laws, for their part, require the fluidity that constitutional laws lack. Providing for the day-to-day administration of the state and regulating the conduct of its people, statutory laws are numerous, detailed, and guided in their development more by everyday empirical conditions than abstract principles. Legislators must be able to enact and amend such laws relatively quickly, for empirical conditions change, and statutory laws need to be able to keep up with the changing world.

If good constitutional laws will be enduring, they need not last forever. When the framers of the Bill of Rights drafted the Second Amendment, it was a wise constitutional provision. The young United States had just freed itself from British tyranny, and the framers did not want to risk slipping back into tyranny at the hands of a government they had invested with power themselves. In England, the citizen militia had long been recognized as one of the best means of checking the power of the central government by serving as a counterweight to the professional army. And the colonial militias had proved the effectiveness of this institution for resisting tyranny by helping to throw off British rule, as enforced by professional British soldiers. Thus, when the framers drafted the Bill of Rights, they agreed to an amendment ensuring the ability of the states to form militias, and of citizens to arm themselves for militia service, thereby erecting a "last-resort" defense against any possible moves toward tyranny by the federal government.

Over the course of two centuries, the United States has matured as a democracy. The democratic institutions the Constitution established, together with the democratic culture these institutions have fostered, have greatly reduced the threat of the federal government tyrannizing over the states. Over this same period, the citizen militia has lost any relevance in American society. The citizen militias, in the sense the framers understood, no longer exist. Nor would a state militia be suited these days to fulfilling the traditional primary duty of militias, defending against foreign invasion and domestic insurgency. With modern warfare depending on weapons systems so complex, expensive, and destructive that citizens training a few times a year could not be entrusted with them, the professional military, including the National Guard, must now take complete responsibility for national and civil defense. And because the military possesses this advanced weaponry, state militias composed of privately armed citizens—if they existed—would no longer provide a credible check against federal tyranny. The rough balance of power that once existed between the militias and the professional military has tipped too radically in favor of the military. But this does not mean a descent into tyranny is now inevitable, for advances in communications technology have vastly enhanced peoples' power to resist repressive governments through largely non-violent means, including strikes, boycotts, civil disobedience, and mass demonstrations.

Taking all of these social and technological changes together, the militia has simply lost its ability to play the institutional role the framers envisioned for it when they drafted the Second Amendment. In other words, the state militias have fallen out of the Constitution's system of checks and balances. Consequently, the right to keep and bear arms for militia service has become antiquated, and the Second Amendment has become obsolete. To make this claim is not to charge the framers with any lack of foresight. They were quite right to focus their attention on the most pressing dangers of the day and to erect the strongest defenses possible against these dangers. Indeed, it is a testament to the political genius of the framers that the democratic system they crafted has matured to a point where it no longer requires the latent threat of mass armed resistance to keep the federal government in check. But this point has been reached. And even if the federal government were somehow to begin moving in the direction of tyranny, the state militias would no longer be the institution to stop it. Hence, in the interest of keeping the Constitution strong by keeping it lean, the Second Amendment should be repealed.

An Insurance Policy?

All of the premises of the above argument might be granted, yet the conclusion denied, as to the advisability of repealing the Second Amendment. Granted, the objection might run, the danger of a tyrannical federal government arising appears quite remote at present. And granted, a citizen militia would face tremendous odds battling a modern professional military. Finally, granted that, in most cases, massive popular protests will now be a more effective means of resisting tyranny than armed struggle. Yet, we cannot be absolutely certain some future federal government will not attempt to tyrannize over the states and the people. And though the state militias would be outgunned by the professional military, if they were to adopt guerilla tactics they might be able to hold out long enough for other pressures to frustrate the government's designs on tyranny. Finally, non-violent means of resistance to a tyrannical federal government may not always prove effective, or even possible, for instance, if the government were to use the army to enforce a ban on public demonstrations. Hence, on the principle of "Better safe than sorry," we should retain the Second Amendment. After all, retaining the amendment does no harm—the desirability of a lean constitution notwithstanding, the Constitution is hardly weakened by the presence of the Third Amendment, a completely antiquated amendment that protects people against having soldiers quartered in their homes. And just maybe, at some point in the unforeseeable future, privately armed citizens forming into militias will prove to be the difference between a tyrannical federal government seizing absolute power and the people successfully defending their liberty. Indeed, the mere thought of a privately armed citizenry may be enough to keep the federal government from ever attempting such a power grab.

In response to this objection, I would concede that we cannot completely rule out the possibility of the federal government, or certain elements within it, attempting to establish a tyranny at some point. Nor can we be sure non-violent means of protest will always prove more effective than armed resistance. I would merely assert that a constitution cannot guard against every possible threat to the state. Consequently, it must make provisions only against only the most likely threats and invoke the safeguards most likely to provide an effective defense. If the Bill of Rights were drawn up today, it would not contain a militia provision, neither the threat against which this institution guards, nor the institution itself having any presence in contemporary American life. Repealing the Second Amendment would reflect these changes in American society, as well as demonstrating the ability of the Constitution to remain a powerful, living, relevant document over the course of centuries.

Perhaps if the Second Amendment had simply slipped into oblivion, like the Third, it would make sense to retain this amendment on the principle of "Better safe than sorry." For it is true that the Third Amendment does not clutter up the Constitution: no one pays any attention to it. The Second Amendment, however, has not similarly slipped out of sight, despite the irrelevance of militias in contemporary America. On the contrary, the Second Amendment is constantly dragged into America's public policy debate on guns by those who interpret the amendment as guaranteeing an unrestricted individual right to bear arms. I have argued that this is not a tenable interpretation of the Second Amendment. Nevertheless, it is at least plausible enough that the Second Amendment will continue to be dragged into the gun debate for as long as it remains part of the Constitution. And this, I would suggest, may be contributing to a threat to our civil rights that is more realistic and more immediate than the threat of a renegade federal government attempting to establish a tyranny.

The Contemporary Threat to Civic Rights

Federal courts have consistently ruled that the Second Amendment does not guarantee an individual right to bear arms for purposes other than militia service. This is appropriate, for the right to bear arms is not a natural right, nor would a constitutionally conferred civic right to bear arms for purposes other than militia service make good sense. To suggest that we have a natural right to bear arms for recreational purposes would be absurd; it would be like claiming we have a natural right to own golf clubs. Equally nonsensical would be a constitutionally conferred right to engage in a few selected forms of recreation, especially when the requisite equipment has the potential to cause great social harm. Entering civil society does not necessarily require that we give up our hunting rifles and target pistols, but constitutionally conferring a right to own such sporting guns would amount to placing one person's enjoyment over another person's life.

A stronger argument can be made for the right to bear arms for self-defense being a natural right. Yet, this argument, too, collapses. Although we do not necessarily give up our freedom to own guns for self-defense when we enter civil society, we may coherently do so. Indeed, it will be irrational for us not to, if we believe restricting gun ownership will maximize the safety of ourselves and others. Consequently, the natural freedom to bear arms for self-defense cannot be an inalienable natural right. Any such right would have to be a constitutionally conferred civic right. A conferred right to bear arms for self-defense would be bad constitutional law, however, for while in some social contexts allowing private gun ownership may enhance public safety, in other situations restricting gun ownership will be the better policy for reducing gun violence. Which public safety strategy will be most effective in any particular situation depends, not on any abstract principles, but on a whole slew of empirical facts—detailed, ever-changing, real-world facts. Constitutionally blocking policy makers from even considering one of the two possible responses to gun violence contradicts the very social contract, for in some cases this may force policy makers to take an approach that the facts indicate will diminish public safety and increase public fearfulness.

In spite of these considerations, and in spite of the federal court rulings, gun advocates still frequently invoke the Second Amendment as an argument against any sort of gun control measures, proclaiming such measures to be unconstitutional. This shifting of the gun debate from the public policy sphere to that of constitutional law is, at best, highly distracting. For supporters of the control measures must then respond with their own constitutional arguments, whether to the effect that the Second Amendment guarantees only a collective right of states to form militias, or that the individual right it invokes only covers gun ownership for militia service. This debate may go back and forth for some time, on a more or less sophisticated level. Meanwhile, however, the truly pressing question has been forgotten: Will the proposed control measures actually reduce gun violence, or will they perhaps lead to an increase in crime or some other social evil?

Dragging the gun debate from the public policy sphere into the constitutional sphere further has the effect of raising passions to a level where objectivity and the free exchange of ideas must suffer. Suddenly, it seems like defending one's own position is tantamount to defending our most cherished liberties, whereas the opposing side must have some sinister, unpatriotic intent. When any debate becomes this emotional and personalized, participants rarely stop to make a cool examination of the facts at hand, or to listen open-mindedly to what the other side has to say.

Finally, when gun policy is made a constitutional issue, compromise becomes nearly impossible. After all, the Constitution is at stake, and constitutional freedoms are not to be compromised away. Officials of the National Rifle Association have been particularly blunt about adopting a "no compromise" stance, resolving to fight even the most modest forms of gun control tooth and nail. This is partly because they fear gun privileges rest on a "slippery slope"—accept a few minor restrictions on guns, and soon the government will enact more restrictions until finally all guns have been confiscated. But compromise is also rejected because many gun advocates sincerely believe they are fighting for the Constitution, itself, viewing the right to bear arms as the guarantor of all other rights. I have argued that this view is mistaken, but given that people hold it, one can hardly blame them for digging in their heels. This hard line, however, has forced pro-control groups like Handgun Control, Inc., to adopt similarly uncompromising stances in favor of gun control. The result is a mutual intransigence, under which conditions it is impossible to craft public policy in the usual democratic fashion—through discussion, compromise, and consensus. Consequently, the United States has not managed to develop a coherent, common sense, middle of the road approach to the problem of gun violence. Instead, the country has two radical, diametrically opposed strategies, both of which are shortsighted and incomplete, and whose proponents spend more time and energy battling one another than the actual problem of gun violence.

So why not keep the Second Amendment around as long as there is the slightest chance a tyrannical federal government will attempt to seize absolute power? The answer is that, whereas in 1789 the greatest threat to civic rights in the United States was that of a would-be tyrant seizing power, this threat has receded and been replaced by another. Imagine for a moment the following scenario, admittedly rather alarmist. Violent crime rates, after falling through the late 1990's, begin to rise again. The Supreme Court, having picked up several conservative justices, overturns *United States v. Miller*. The majority opinion holds that the Second Amendment does guarantee an unrestricted individual right to bear arms, and moreover, that it protects individuals against state and local gun restrictions as well as against federal restrictions. Hence, gun control has essentially become unconstitutional. Realizing they cannot hope to reduce the number of guns in circulation, governments on all levels begin encouraging law-abiding citizens to acquire guns, hoping a well-armed populace will deter crime. And, in fact, this policy does steer some potential criminals into more productive lives.

Other criminals, however, feel the public has declared war on them, and they move to defend themselves. Criminals begin acquiring more powerful guns, which they begin using, not just to commit other crimes but sometimes simply to intimidate the public. Furthermore, with so many victims turning out to be armed, most criminals adopt a policy of "Shoot first, ask questions later." Hence, the number of gun crimes goes up, and the crimes committed become more violent. In response, more and more law-abiding citizens decide they need to carry guns, and they buy guns with ever-greater firepower, trying to keep up with the criminals. Moreover, as citizens begin losing confidence in the state's ability to protect them, they begin taking responsibility, not just for defending themselves but for exacting retribution against known criminals. By this point, a war is breaking out between law-abiding citizens and criminals, with each side continually increasing its firepower, and getting more ruthless in its tactics. Yet, the distinction between "law-abiding" and "criminal" begins to break down, for the vigilante justice being practiced is itself extralegal, so all the fighting is now taking place beyond the bounds of civil society. Ultimately, everyone simply fights for his or her own protection, paying no attention to the laws of the state. A Hobbesian war of all against all has erupted; civil society has collapsed. People once again enjoy all the freedoms they enjoyed in the state of nature. But they have also lost all the civic freedoms they attained within civil society, including freedom from the ever-present fear of violent death.

Granted, the United States is not likely to slide back into the state of nature in this fashion, even if violent crime levels should skyrocket. The American political system and democratic culture are strong enough that the country would not allow itself to descend into anarchy without taking counteractive measures. But we must consider what measures the nation might take to head off such a slide if gun violence levels began to rise again, or even if gun deaths continue to drop, but the public fear level continued to rise as the mass media pump images of ever more sensational gun crimes into our living rooms. At some point, calls will be put out for the government to do more to ensure public safety. People will demand, not just that the courts impose harsher sentences on convicted criminals but that police do more to deter and preempt gun crimes. And police *can* do more to head off gun violence—by stepping up their general presence and adopting tactics that law-abiding citizens and criminals alike will find unpleasantly invasive. This will cause some misgivings, but if the public safety crisis continues to intensify, police will find themselves encouraged to adopt tactics which, if they do not actually violate peoples' civic rights, begin pressing up against them. Especially vulnerable are Fourth Amendment protections against unreasonable searches and seizures. These protections are not absolute; the framers realized such police tactics would sometimes need to be used, and thus were careful to protect only against "unreasonable" searches and seizures. As the violent crime rate goes higher, more invasive searches for illegal weapons or other criminal paraphernalia will be deemed reasonable, not just by police and courts, but by the general public. This may not amount to the emergence of a police state, but it does constitute a very real scaling back of civic rights.

Would such an erosion of civic rights occur if the Supreme Court reinterpreted the Second Amendment as guaranteeing an unrestricted individual right to bear arms? I do not know, but it is possible. Indeed, I believe it is conceivable we could enter onto such a path even if we remain at the status quo, where the courts strictly limit Second Amendment protections to the context of militia service, but a public generally unaware of this allows the public policy debate on guns to be continually dragged into the constitutional sphere. For this sidetracks and polarizes the public policy debate so badly that it prevents lawmakers from crafting a coherent strategy to reduce gun violence. Without a coherent national strategy, it is unlikely the country will ever reduce gun violence to a tolerable level. And fear of gun violence could lead us to accept limitations on our civic rights in the interest of winning greater safety.

Indeed, policy makers have already found it necessary to take some measured, yet real, steps toward bolstering public safety, at the cost of greater police intrusiveness. Consider what has happened in schools. A rash of school shootings in the late 1990's left children and parents terrified. In response, many schools began employing armed guards, installing metal detectors, and searching student lockers more frequently. Some students have complained that such measures make them feel like Big Brother is watching. The general consensus, however, is that the threat to student safety justifies these impositions. It is difficult to know what measures the next school shooting will prompt or what measures factories and office buildings will start adopting the next time a disgruntled employee goes on a shooting spree. We cannot foresee how many restrictions Americans will accept on their civic liberties when they fear for their lives. But we must certainly say the threat to civic rights coming from this direction is currently far greater, and far more realistic, than the threat of the federal government establishing a tyranny.

Political thinkers going back to the ancient Greeks have realized the greatest threat to a democracy is not that a dictator will come to forcibly impose himself on the people. The greatest threat is that the people, themselves—seeing their society disintegrate into a chaotic battle of self-interested individuals—will install a tyrant over themselves. According to the classic cycle of governments, monarchies tend to transform into oligarchies as more people demand a share of the power. The masses then become unhappy at being ruled by the few, so the oligarchy gradually transforms itself into a democracy. A democracy state may endure for a time, but as individual citizens invested with power for the first time begin madly using it to advance their own interests, the society begins to slide into anarchy. Gripped with fear at the ensuing mayhem, the people latch onto the first strong leader they find and beg him to take power so as to restore order.

When the United States embarked on its experiment in government, skeptics at home and in Europe believed the young country would soon go this route, placing itself back under the British crown or establishing a homegrown dictatorship within a generation. Two centuries later, the United States has thus far been able to break the cycle of governments. This is mainly because its founders devised a brilliant system of government that spreads power out among many different individuals and institutions—and in a real sense among the entire citizenry—while still allowing for effective governance. Today, it is scarcely conceivable that a dictator could seize power in the United States through an armed coup or that the federal government as a whole would start tyrannizing over the states or the people. These are the kind of threats against which the state citizen militias may once have provided a good defense. The more realistic threat the United States now faces is that the people, themselves, facing intolerable levels of violent crime, will begin calling for limitations on their own civil liberties, in the interest of public safety. I am not suggesting Americans will begin clamoring for a dictator. But people may start demanding that the government play a stronger role in combating gun violence, even if this entails a more intrusive police presence or other measures that whittle down civic rights. Such a loss of civic freedom will be regrettable, yet Americans may well judge it worth the gains made in public safety if gun violence cannot be reduced by any other means. And without a coherent national strategy to combat gun violence, the country has little chance of bringing gun violence down to a tolerable level.

Insofar as the Second Amendment is one factor that hinders the development of a coherent national strategy to reduce gun violence, it contributes to the danger that Americans will themselves give up some of their civic liberties in the interest of public safety. This danger is far more real today than the threat of the federal government attempting to tyrannize over the states. Hence, as contributing to a threat more pressing than the threat against which it guards, the Second Amendment should be repealed.

*   *   *   *   *   *   *

Would tighter gun restrictions reduce gun violence? Or is promoting gun ownership a more effective strategy for deterring crime? Is some sort of compromise approach possible? I honestly do not know the answer to these questions. But I do know that if policy makers are to craft an effective gun strategy, they must have the policy options of both gun control and legal gun ownership open to them. I would also maintain that we cannot hope to craft a coherent strategy in the present political atmosphere, with statutory and constitutional issues constantly getting confused, passions running so high that objective debate is impossible, the spirit of compromise having been long since lost. Repealing the Second Amendment would not instantly create an atmosphere more conducive to constructive debate on the gun issue. Indeed, the fight over repeal would be the battle of all gun battles, doubtless resolving itself into a polarized clash between the gun lobby and the gun control lobby. Once again, however, it must be stressed that the argument for repeal is not an argument for gun control. Repeal would not, of itself, place any restrictions on gun ownership, nor would it establish a political atmosphere necessarily more favorable to gun control than to gun privileges. Repeal of the Second Amendment would merely locate the gun debate more securely in its proper forum, that of statutory, not constitutional, law. If the Second Amendment can be repealed, then one hopes, once the wounds from the constitutional battle have healed, the gun debate can be re-entered in more focused, sober, and conciliatory fashion, with participants on all sides concentrating exclusively on the urgent question of how best to reduce gun violence.

NOTES

Introduction

1 In 1998, the most recent year for which complete statistics were available at time of publication, the Centers for Disease Control reported 30,708 firearm deaths. *National Vital Statistics Reports*, Vol. 48, No. 11, Jul 24, 2000, p. 68. Gun deaths have been consistently declining since 1994. In 1993, the CDC reported a peak number of 39,595 firearm deaths. *Ibid.* p. 71.
2 The CDC reported 12,102 firearm homicides in 1998. *Ibid.*, p. 68.

Chapter 1: Constitutional and Statutory Law

1 The state legislatures can also originate the amendment process by calling for a constitutional convention; see Article V of the Constitution.
2 Lev 7:22; Lev 19:26, Revised Standard Version.
3 Peters, William, *A More Perfect Union* (New York: Crown Publishers, 1987), p. 137.

Chapter 2: The Right to Bear Arms: English Origins

1 Malcolm, Joyce Lee, *To Keep and Bear Arms: The Origins of an Anglo-American Right* (Cambridge, Mass.: Harvard, 1994), p. ix. Most of the claims regarding gun ownership in this chapter are based on the work of Malcolm. Readers should be aware, however, that Michael Bellesiles has recently called into question the scholarship of Malcolm and others, arguing that privately owned guns were much less prevalent in seventeenth-century England than suggested here. See Bellesiles, Michael A., *Arming America: The Origins of a National Gun Culture* (New York: Alfred A. Knopf, 2000), pp. 17-39.

2 Schwoerer, Lois, *The Declaration of Rights, 1689* (Baltimore: Johns Hopkins Univ. Press, 1981), p. 100.
3 Schwoerer, p. 78.

Chapter 3: The Social Contract and Natural Rights

1 Hobbes, Thomas, *Leviathan*, C.B. Macpherson, ed. (London: Penguin Books, 1968), Ch. 13, p. 62 (original pagination).
2 Hobbes, Ch. 13, p. 62.
3 Hobbes, Ch. 17, p. 85.
4 Locke, John, *Two Treatises of Government*, Mark Goldie, ed. (London: Everyman, 1993), *Second Treatise*, Ch. 2, p. 117.

Chapter 4: The Right to Bear Arms: American Origins

1 Malcolm, p. 139.
2 Bellesiles, p. 106.
3 See esp. Bellesiles, p. 93-103.
4 Bellesiles, p. 121.
5 This power of judicial review is actually not mentioned in the Constitution. The Supreme Court first asserted in 1803 in the case of *Marbury vs. Madison*.
6 Peters, p. 158.
7 *Creating the Bill of Rights: The Documentary Record from the First Federal Congress*, Helen E. Veit, Kenneth R. Bowling, Charlene Bangs Bickford, eds. (Baltimore: Johns Hopkins Univ. Press, 1991), p. 12.
8 *Creating the Bill of Rights*, p. 182.

Chapter 5: Interpreting the Second Amendment

1 *United States v. Tot* (1942), *Cases v. United States* (1942), *United States v. Synnes* (1971).

Chapter 6: The Right to Bear Arms for Militia Service

1 Malcolm, p. 157.
2 Halbrook, Stephen, *That Every Man Be Armed: The Evolution of a Constitutional Right* (Albuquerque: Univ. of New Mexico, 1984), p. 76.
3 Halbrook, p. 77.

4 Blackstone, William, *Commentaries on the Laws of England*, 4 vols. (Chicago: University of Chicago Press, 1979), I:136.
5 Halbrook, p. 74.
6 Madison, James, *The Federalist Papers*, No. 46, Clinton Rossiter, ed. (New York: Mentor, 1999), p. 267.

Further Reading

Following are some suggestions for further reading, arranged roughly according to the chapters of this book. It should be noted that this list represents only a small sampling of the books available that address the questions raised here. Recent books dealing with the contemporary gun debate, in particular, are numerous. The section of this list devoted to the contemporary gun debate includes only books that specifically address the constitutional aspects of gun policy.

The History of the Right to Bear Arms in England

Joyce Lee Malcolm, *To Keep and Bear Arms: The Origins of an Anglo-American Right* (Cambridge, Massachusetts: Harvard University Press, 1994).

P.B. Munsche, *Gentlemen and Poachers* (New York: Cambridge University Press, 1981).

Lois Schwoerer, *The Declaration of Rights, 1689* (Baltimore: Johns Hopkins University Press, 1981).

The Social Contract and Natural Right

William Blackstone, *Commentaries on the Laws of England.*

Thomas Hobbes, *Leviathan.*

Michael Lessnoff, *Social Contract* (London: Macmillan, 1986).

John Locke, *Two Treatises of Government.*

Christopher W. Morris, ed., *The Social Contract Theorists* (Lanham, Maryland: Rowman and Littlefield, 1999).

Jean Jacques Rousseau, *The Social Contract.*

The History of the American Constitution and Bill of Rights

Akhil Reed Amar, *The Bill of Rights: Creation and Reconstruction* (New Haven: Yale University Press, 1998).

Charlene Bangs Bickford, Kenneth R. Bowling, Helen E. Veit, eds., *Creating the Bill of Rights: The Documentary Record from the First Federal Congress* (Baltimore: Johns Hopkins University Press, 1991).

Alexander Hamilton, John Jay, James Madison, *The Federalist Papers.*

Leonard Levy, *Origins of the Bill of Rights* (New Haven: Yale University Press, 1999).

Richard B. Morris, *The Forging of the Union* (New York: Harper and Row, 1987).

William Peters, *A More Perfect Union* (New York: Crown Publishers, 1987).

The History of the Right to Bear Arms in America

Michael A. Bellesiles, *Arming America: The Origins of a National Gun Culture* (New York: Alfred A. Knopf, 2000).

Marjolijn Bijlefeld, *The Gun Control Debate: A Documentary History* (Westport, Connecticut: Greenwood Press, 1997).

Saul Cornell, ed., *Whose Right to Bear Arms Did the Second Amendment Protect?* (Boston: Bedford/St. Martin's, 2000).

Stephen Halbrook, *That Every Man Be Armed: The Evolution of a Constitutional Right* (Albuquerque: University of New Mexico Press, 1984).

John K. Mahon, *History of the Militia and the National Guard* (New York: Macmillan, 1983).

David E. Young, ed., *The Origin of the Second Amendment: A Documentary History of the Bill of Rights in Commentaries on Liberty, Free Government, and an Armed Populace, 1787–1792* (Ontonagon, Michigan: Golden Oak Books, 1995).

The Contemporary Gun Debate

Robert J. Cottrol, ed., *Gun Control and the Constitution: Sources and Explorations* (New York: Garland, 1993).

Jan E. Dizard, Robert Merrill Muth, Stephen P. Andrews, eds., *Guns in America: A Reader* (New York: New York University Press, 1999).

Wilbur Edel, *Gun Control: Threat to Liberty or Defense Against Anarchy?* (Westport, Connecticut: Praeger, 1995).

Don B. Kates, *Guns, Murders, and the Constitution: A Realistic Assessment of Gun Control* (San Francisco: Pacific Research Institute for Public Policy, 1990).

Wayne LaPierre, *Guns, Crime and Freedom* (Washington, D.C.: Regnery, 1994).

Michael A. Sommers, *The Right to Bear Arms* (New York: Rosen Publishing Group, 2000).

Robert J. Spitzer, *The Politics of Gun Control* (New York: Chatham House, 1998).

Joel Sugarmann, *Every Handgun Is Aimed at You: The Case for Banning Handguns* (New York: The New York Press, 2001).

William J. Vizzard, *Shots in the Dark: The Policy, Politics, and Symbolism of Gun Control* (Lanham, Maryland: Rowman and Littlefield, 2000).

William Weir, *A Well Regulated Militia: The Battle over Gun Control* (New Haven: Archon Books, 1997).

INDEX

Teaching Texts in Law and Politics

David Schultz, *General Editor*

The new series Teaching Texts in Law and Politics is devoted to textbooks that explore the multidimensional and multidisciplinary areas of law and politics. Special emphasis will be given to textbooks written for the undergraduate classroom. Subject matters to be addressed in this series include, but will not be limited to: constitutional law; civil rights and liberties issues; law, race, gender, and gender orientation studies; law and ethics; women and the law; judicial behavior and decision-making; legal theory; comparative legal systems; criminal justice; courts and the political process; and other topics on the law and the political process that would be of interest to undergraduate curriculum and education. Submission of single-author and collaborative studies, as well as collections of essays are invited.

Authors wishing to have works considered for this series should contact:

> Peter Lang Publishing
> Acquisitions Department
> 275 Seventh Avenue, 28th floor
> New York, New York 10001

To order other books in this series, please contact our Customer Service Department at:

> 800-770-LANG (within the U.S.)
> (212) 647-7706 (outside the U.S.)
> (212) 647-7707 FAX

or browse online by series at:

> WWW.PETERLANGUSA.COM